THE LIFE AND MARIOLOGY OF FATHER JUNIPER B. CAROL, O.F.M.

By: Chris Padgett

LITTLE RED HOUSE
PUBLISHING

Authored by Chris Padgett

Cover design by Bob Perron. Interior design by Lisa Perron.

Copy editing by Lisa Perron.

Pictures from the Marian Library archives at the International Marian Research Institute in Dayton, Ohio.

TABLE OF CONTENTS

INTRODUCTION

Fr. Juniper B. Carol, O.F.M.

1

THE LIFE AND MARIOLOGY OF FATHER JUNIPER B. CAROL. O.F.M

1.1. General Intent

This work, "The Life and Mariology of Father Juniper B. Carol, O.F.M.," will examine Carol's time as a Franciscan who spent a great portion of his life working, publishing, and living independent from his community and its traditional expectations of a highly educated friar. This unique way of living afforded him the opportunity to spend significant time publishing books and spearheading the formation and organization of the Mariological Society of America. This study will also examine his role in three Marian teachings upon which Carol regularly focused. The first is the absolute primacy and predestation of Jesus and His Virgin Mother,[1] the second is the "*debitum peccati*"[2] and the last is Mary as Coredemptrix.[3] Much of Carol's comprehensive Mariology will spring from these three themes, such as the connection with Mary's Queenship and its relationship to Coredemption. Carol writes, "Her claim to be styled Queen, at least with regard to the human race, rests on something more real than a figure of speech; it is a necessary consequence of her proximate cooperation in the

---

[1] *The Absolute Primacy and Predestination of Jesus and His Virgin Mother*, is the title of his book published with Franciscan Herald Press, Chicago, IL, in 1981.

[2] In general, the *debitum peccati* may be defined as "the universal necessity to contract original sin." Rev. Juniper Carol, O.F.M. *A History of the Controversy Over the "Debitum Peccati*," in *Franciscan Institute Publications;* Theology Series No. 9, ed. George Marcil, O.F.M. (Bonaventure, NY, The Franciscan Institute of St. Bonaventure University, 1978), 4.

[3] Unless placed within a quote, the word Coredemptrix will be capitalized and written without the hyphen for consistency.

2

work of our Redemption"[4] Moreover, as noted by Father Peter D. Fehlner in his 1992 article "Fr. Juniper B. Carol, O.F.M.: *His Mariology and Scholarly Achievement.,"* each of these Marian themes fits within the broader category of mediation,[5] which according to Fehlner includes the distribution of graces and Mary's participation in their acquisition.

While many lay persons may not immediately recognize Father Juniper Carol's name, or even much about his Mariology, students of Mariology will find this Franciscan priest cited frequently in academic and popular publications. Marian theologians such as Dr. Mark Miravalle,[6] Father Peter Fehlner,[7] and Msgr. Arthur Burton Calkins,[8] to name a few, all refer to Carol and his publications. Dr. Mark Miravalle regularly requires texts referencing Father Carol for his university classes at Franciscan University of Steubenville. After reading this analysis of Carol's life and Mariology, many will find a greater appreciation of Marian devotion grounded in the Church and our Lord Jesus Christ.

---

4   Juniper B. Carol, "The Mariological Movement in the World Today." *Marian Studies* 1 (1950): 44

5   As Fehlner states, "…and the then general interest throughout the Church in the theme of Our Lady's mediation (not only her role in the distribution of graces, but also her sharing in their acquisition as Coredemptrix) played a part." Peter D. Fehlner, O.F.M. Conv., "Fr. Juniper B. Carol, O.F.M.: His Mariology and Scholarly Achievement.*" Marian Studies* 43 (Dayton, OH, The Mariological Society of America, 1992): 18.

6   One example of using Carol's work is found in a chapter written by Dr. Miravalle and Rev. John A. Schug, O.F.M.Cap called, "Mary, Coredemptrix: The Significance of Her Title in the Magisterium of The Church". The book is, *Mary Coredemptrix Mediatrix Advocate: Theological Foundations Towards a Papal Definition?* (Goleta, CA, Queenship Publishing, 1995), 215.

7   See *St. Maximilian M. Kolbe, Martyr of Charity; Pneumatologist: His Theology of the Holy Spirit* (New Bedford, MA: Academy Of The Immaculate, 2004), 185.

8   Arthur B. Calkins, "Mary Co-Redemptrix: The Beloved Associate of Christ", *Mariology A Guide for Priests, Deacons, Seminarians, and Consecrated Persons.* (Santa Barbara, CA, Seat of Wisdom Books: A Division of Queenship Publishing, 2007), 378.

The life of Father Carol is quite fascinating. From his early years in Cuba, to his scholarly work in Rome, eventual assignments in academia, the starting of the Mariological Society of America, to his pastoral and published ministry, and finally his death, Carol's life is an example of the impact one individual can have within a field of theological study.

The heightened interest in Marian theology in the first half of the twentieth century was salutary for Father Carol's career.[9] And his work continues to resonate in the twenty-first century with many in Mariology today,[10] to those who are sympathetic towards him and even those who are not.[11] For Carol, his understanding of his Christian faith included Mary. In fact, he thought that Christianity only made sense when Mary was seen in her rightful place. Carol once wrote: "Christianity with Mary in her rightful place is the only Christianity that makes sense."[12]

---

[9] Father Manelli writes, "'It has been authoritatively asserted by T. Koehler that the twentieth century has been a 'century of Mariology.' More precisely, perhaps, one could say that the twentieth century has been the century of 'co-redemptionists,' and in particular of the Saints and Blessed, Venerable and Servants of God, all upholding the Co-redemption, loving and singing, venerating and defending that so delightful truth of Marian Co-redemption with speech and writing, virtues and works, veneration and devotion." 257–58. Rev. Stefano Manelli, F.F.I. "Marian Coredemption in the Hagiography of the 20th Century." *Mary Co-redemptrix Doctrinal Issues Today*, (Goleta, CA, Queenship Publishing, 2002), 257–58. Manelli is not necessarily accurate in saying that Koehler thought the 20th century was the century of Coredemption. 1830-1950 is usually seen as the Marian century.

[10] Such as Father Manelli, F.F.I., and other Mariologists such as Dr. Miravalle, Father Peter Fehlner, and Msgr. Calkins.

[11] In support of Carol, see Mark Miravalle, *Introduction to Mary*, (Goleta, CA, Queenship Publishing, 1993), 51–82. Specifically, endnotes 2, 5, and 9 in above cited work where Miravalle refers to Carol who speaks of Mary as "Spiritual Mother, "Meriting more graces than any other created person.," and "Dispensatrix of all graces". 62,69,75.

[12] Father Juniper B. Carol, O.F.M., *Mariology* 3, (Milwaukee, The Bruce Publishing Company, 1961), vii.

It is important to note that Carol's Mariology was always at its core a direct application of his Christianity.

This thesis will look at Father Carol's life more thoroughly than any other written work, making references to what has been previously published. The Franciscan influence upon Carol's Mariology will also be examined, including his 1948 appointment to the Marian Commission as the Secretary General for the United States to the International Franciscan Commission, a position he held for twenty years.[13] The biography will explore his origins in Cuba, his education as a young boy at Tusculum College in Tennessee, and his attendance at St. Joseph's in Havana, Cuba. This study will look at his involvement with the Franciscans, the Order of Friars Minor of the Holy Name Province, giving mention to members of his order and those who knew Carol personally. His doctoral work on Coredemption was done in Rome, and in 1949, Father Juniper started the Mariological Society of America, which is still in existence today. Carol's passion for Mariology is well documented in his publications by the Mariological Society of America. The biography will show that Father Carol lived a rather unique life, that often separated him from his province. His devotion and fidelity to the Church, to the Franciscans, and to Our Lady is without question.

1.2. Status Quaestionis

The life of Father Carol is not widely known outside of *The Provincial Annals* and online information found at the Holy Name Province. Nor can much be gleaned from the few

---

[13] *The Provincial Annals*, "Another Friar Named to Marian Commission," VI (New York, NY, Holy Name Province, 1947-48): 301. Which says, "Father Juniper Carol, a friar of Holy Name Province, who is at present attached to the Pontifical University of St. Anthony, Rome, was appointed Secretary General for the United States of the International Franciscan Commission of Mariology."

accounts in *Marian Studies*, giving a brief biography of Father Juniper B. Carol by then President, James McCurry, O.F.M. Conv. "Fr. Juniper B. Carol, O.F.M., 1911–1990: *Vir Catholicus Et Totus Apostolicus.*" *Marian Studies* 42 *(*1991): 9-14., and a written homage to the founder of the Mariological Society of America by Theodore A. Koehler, S.M.: "In Homage to the Founder of the Mariological Society of America Juniper Benjamin Carol., O.F.M. (1911–1990)." *Ephemerides Mariologiae*, Annus LIII-Fasc.II-n.142, (Rome, 1991), 709-713.; therefore, there was a need for a careful study of his life while living witnesses remain to give a first-hand account concerning this friar. I have investigated all published accounts in English concerning Carol's life, working in collaboration with the librarian at Bonaventure College, who allowed me some access to archives referencing Carol. In addition, I have done phone and email interviews gathering unique first-hand reflections about Father Juniper and studied published material available on the life of Carol. This work aspires to be a useful contribution to both Mariology as well as to the remembrance of a Franciscan friar whose entire life was given to promoting Marian studies. Jessica Catherine Kozack wrote the most recent treatment of Carol's Mariology in her master's thesis for the University of Dayton, Ohio. Her work is entitled, "The Primacy of Christ as the Foundation of the Co-redemption: The Mariology of Fr. Juniper B. Carol, O.F.M" (1911-1990). (Aug. 2015) and will be referenced throughout this study. Kozack focuses more on showing the underpinnings of Carol's Mariology, namely the relationship between Thomistic and Scotistic thought. She presents a big picture of Mariology during the time in which Carol lived and does an excellent job placing her thesis on Carol within the context of Marian study before and after Vatican II. Kozack writes,

His work is important both because it provides an example of the thought of an American Franciscan theologian of the twentieth century and because Carol had a major influence on international Mariology, making it worthwhile to consider how he responded to the changes in Mariology after Vatican II.[14]

While I appreciate her perspective, and will reference it where needed, I am going to show that Carol is not the originator of a new idea or a personal Mariology; rather, what Carol gives is a masterful synthesis of all the varying views on the Marian topics of Coredemption, the *debitum peccati* and the absolute primacy and Predestination of Jesus and His Virgin Mother. Carol represents each of these topics as fairly as possible, gathering and cataloging all publications on said topic, but leaning as a general rule towards the Franciscan perspective.

1.3.   Structure

In this study the structure is more of a narrative. Beginning with a brief historical and political context for Father Carol's biography, this will lead into an overview of the Franciscans and take us into the Mariological explanation of Carol's work. This thesis will show the Marian perspective of the time in which Carol lived, both the ecclesial and cultural. This thesis will also show specific examples of Franciscan life and expectations from the order to which Carol belonged. The thesis will offer the reader unique contributions concerning this friar, namely, information concerning specific classes and information about his attendance as a youth at Tusculum

---

[14]   Kozack, Jessica Catherine, *The Primacy of Christ as the Foundation of the Co-redemption: The Mariology of Fr. Juniper B. Carol, O.F.M. (1911-1990).* (Aug. 2015). Pg. 1.

7

College in Tennessee, along with some interviews by religious who have remembrances of having known Father Carol, either as a student or fellow friar. Carol's unique independence from his Franciscan community may bespeak a subtle tension between him and his community, which Father Dominic Monti, who has been the Provincial Vicar of the Holy Name Province since 2005, alludes to in an interview I had with him on 1/30/13.[15] Monti says concerning Carol:

> For the second half of his life—the part I would have known—he was really on the fringes of our Province. I certainly believe he was out of sympathy with theological trends and directions in the Province following Vatican II and was somewhat isolated in ministries of his own choosing. If you see from his biography, he served in various chaplaincies and other such 'one-man' assignments after 1967, living on his own—he moved into our friary in St Petersburg only in 1979. I know many older friars considered him somewhat of a prima donna, and one who did not 'pitch in' with the ministries other friars were engaged in. To them he seemed to take pride in a certain aristocratic (?) background that set him apart from the hoi polloi. In other words, he was never a 'community man.' Now, one must also say that the province during the 40s, 50s, 60s and 70s was dominated by an Irish and Italian crowd from the Northeast (New England, New York, New Jersey, Pennsylvania), the sons of largely first and second generation immigrants, so there

---

[15] See Appendix C for the full content of this interview.

may have been a certain amount of prejudice on their part against this Latino. But my definite impression from them is that Juniper considered himself 'special,' a trait they disliked.[16]

While Monti notes some of the reasons for the tensions, Carol was never disobedient to his superiors or the Church.

This thesis will finally explore the three previously mentioned Mariological areas Father Carol did most of his publishing and exploration in: The Predestination of Our Lady with her Son, the *Debitum Peccati,* and Mary as Coredemptrix.

1.4. Method

Looking at what is in *Marian Studies*, Carol's books, and published articles, as well as gaining first-hand accounts about Carol, and the Mariological orientation of his work, this thesis moves from a biographical and historical analysis to a theological and Mariological methodology. This thesis maintains an emphasis on the publications for which Father Carol was most known. His membership in the Franciscan order will offer insight into why certain Mariological areas are of greater interest to Carol than others. This study will note the overall Mariological context of his life.

1.5. Limitations

My greatest limitation for this dissertation is the fact that there are so few living witnesses who can attest to the personal character and devotional life of Father Carol. It has been suggested to me by Father Fehlner that there was a lengthy and insightful correspondence between Father Carol and Father

---

[16] Email with Father Dominic Monti on 1/30/13.

Balic during the time of the Second Vatican Council; however, I have not been able to find these letters as of yet.[17] These limitations could be offset in future biographical works with the discovery of such correspondence and any personal journals from students of Fr. Carol, but do not hinder the substance of this thesis by not being included. The only other limitation I had in my work was a lack of correspondence to me from the seminary in Havana, Cuba that Carol attended as a child. After reaching out they simply did not, either find anything of use available on Carol, or consider my request to be a priority meriting a response. This lack of correspondence with the seminary is of minor importance for the thesis.

---

[17]   This is based on phone correspondence I had on 8/14/2012 with Father Peter Fehlner.

The Franciscan and Mariological Context

Father Juniper Carol O.F.M. and Fr. Cyril Vollert S.J.

11

Father Juniper Carol, O.F.M. worked and resided in Cuba, Italy and the United States from August of 1930 until his death in April of 1990. His religious order was The Holy Name Province Order of Friars, a Franciscan order located in Bonaventure, New York, with its Provincial Office in New York, NY.[18] It is now the largest of the seven OFM provinces in the United States.[19]

1.6.   Franciscan Context

Carol belonged to the Franciscan Friars of the Holy Name Province which had a strong missionary zeal in ministering to Catholic immigrants. Author, Joseph White wrote a history of the Holy Name Province, encompassing the time frame between the 1950's until 2004. Mr. White writes:

> Responding to their Franciscan call to mission, Father Pamfilo de Magliano and three other friars came from Italy to western New York in 1855. There they strove to meet the needs of Catholic immigrants. Soon they were staffing parishes and educating lay men and diocesan seminarians at St. Bonaventure's College and Seminary.

---

[18]   See, The Holy Name Province website for more information: https://hnp.org/who-we-are/our-province/ As of 3/25/2019.

[19]   "More than a century later, we are now the largest of the seven OFM provinces in the United States. Based in New York City, we have friaries in Massachusetts, Connecticut, New York, New Jersey, Pennsylvania, Delaware, Maryland, Virginia, the Carolinas, Georgia and Florida. Individual friars also serve in various other U.S. locations and as missionaries in South America and Asia, mostly working with other Franciscan entities." https://hnp.org/who-we-are/our-province/ As of 3/29/2019.

Though not strictly consistent with earlier Franciscan tradition, these ministries grew out of the needs of the time and place: America's immigrant church. The Franciscans' presence and work would lead to the formation of the Custody of the Immaculate Conception.[20]

The work of these Franciscans would grow and flourish over the years with Father Carol joining the friars novitiate in 1930 at the age of twenty. The emphasis on catechesis for seminarians and lay men was part of the charism of these New York-based friars, and as a result the friary became a fitting place for Carol, who would spend his life's work in publishing Mariology for the faithful's spiritual growth.

While mission work and catechesis were part of Father Pamfilo's original intentions for the order, as demonstrated by their coming to America and educating seminarians according to White's work on the Friars Minor, the mutual bond between the friars was an essential part of the labor and order. Yet the personality of Father Carol was such that the desire to advance Mariology and retain a connection with his Franciscan religious community would prove to be difficult.

Carol's study and work habit was often gathering material by Mariologists and sharing the Franciscan perspective in matters dealing with Coredemption and the debt of sin. He was also very diligent in giving a proper view of the Thomistic position in his synthesis since this was being highlighted in theology. Jessica Catherine Kozack notes that while there was an emphasis on Thomism encouraged by Pope Leo XIII and

---

[20] Joseph M. White, *Peace and Good in America, A History of Holy Name Province Order of Friars Minor 1850s To The Present*. (New York, NY, Holy Name Province, 2004), 3.

Pius X, the Franciscans adhered to their own theological pedigree. This was the heritage Carol was part of. Kozack writes:

> Despite the papal emphasis on Thomism, Franciscans continued to value their own intellectual heritage. For example, a 1953 article from *Franciscan Studies* stated, 'Not each and every portion of Aquinas's philosophical system has the same eternal value.' One can disagree with Aquinas and still be in agreement with the Church; Aquinas does not have a 'quasi-infallibility.' This defensive stance that seeks to prove Franciscan ideas are in harmony with the teaching of the Church will shape Carol's work, even after the Council.[21]

The Franciscan order was a great part of who Father Carol was as a priest and Marxologist. Here are a few Franciscan commissions and congresses to keep in mind. The International Franciscan Commission on Mariology is important because Carol became the Secretary General for the United States on January 4, 1948. The Very Reverend Charles Balic was the Director General of this Commission during this time which covered the whole order. There are also Marian Congresses held in places like Portugal, Italy and Spain, with events planned for Canada and Latin America during 1948. When the Marian Congress is held in the United States it is called a National Marian Congress.[22] The Franciscan Marian Commission was a local group, as well as the National Marian

---

[21] Kozack, *The Primacy of Christ as the Foundation of the Co-redemption*, 14-15.

[22] See, *The Provincial Annals*, "Another Friar Named to Marian Commission," VI (New York, NY, Holy Name Province, 1947-48): 302.

Council, which has six members representing six provinces. One event of note was the Marian Commission, which had a national and international impact as it shared through scholarship the privileges of Mary. White writes, "The province participated in the National Marian Commission, formed in 1947 as a unit of the Franciscan Marian Commission organized by the general minister."[23] This Commission was largely at work in furthering the continued understanding of the Immaculate Conception, with a specific purpose of achieving four goals: First, to describe its history in every province, second, to honor Mary's highest prerogative in every nation, third, to publish a three-part work on the dogma and its art and history, and finally to exhibit in Rome an international exposition illustrating its truths.[24] *The Provincial Annals* articulate the purpose of the International Franciscan Marian Commission of Mariology as, "the more apt and scientific elucidation of each and every prerogative of the blessed Virgin, in preparation for the centennial celebration in 1954 of the dogmatic definition of the Immaculate Conception."[25] The local congresses were given a different focus; that of the Assumption. "The various national congresses will deal in particular with the death and Assumption of the Blessed Virgin with a view to the ultimate dogmatic definition of the Assumption by Holy Mother the Church."[26] White continues, "Representatives of the six United States provinces made up the National Marian Commission. Father Berard Vogt represented Holy Name Province. Later the province's Father Juniper Carol was appointed directly by Fr. Mathias, who was the procurator

---

23 See White, *Peace and Good in America*, 291.
24 See White, *Peace and Good in America*, 291.
25 *The Provincial Annals*, "Another Friar Named to Marian Commission," VI (New York, NY, Holy Name Province, 1947-48): 302.
26 *The Provincial Annals*, "Another Friar Named to Marian Commission," 302.

general."[27] This was an ongoing commission that would also have a provincial Marian council established for local Marian events. One example was the Marian Day held on December 9, 1948 for the young clerics of St. Anthony Friary.[28] Father Carol's work for the Franciscan Marian Commission of his order, the Mariological Society of America, and his numerous publications were certainly sympathetic to the heritage of Franciscan theology. Carol would continue to focus on Mary's Immaculate Conception, matters of sin and also Mary as Mediatrix.

Carol wanted an association, "to promote an exchange of views on Marian doctrines and to further studies and research in Mariology."[29] He addressed in the first issue of *Marian Studies* the Mariological Movement in the world within which he lived. He was clear about what this meant concerning the Mariological situation of his time: "By 'Mariological Movement' is meant here the various manifestations of Catholic theological thought in its endeavor to expound and elucidate the prerogatives of the Mother of God in a scientific manner."[30] His work in Coredemption especially fulfills this mission to exchange views on Marian doctrine and is an enhancement of the Franciscan commitment to promote the Immaculate Conception.

1.7.   General Marian Overview in America leading up to Carol's time:

In 1930, Benjamin Carol came to America to be received into the Franciscan order as a novitiate. When Carol arrived in the United States, he found enthusiasm for

---

27 White, *Peace and Good in America*, 291.
28 See White, *Peace and Good in America*, 291.
29 Carol, "The Mariological Movement in the World Today." 17.
30 Carol, "The Mariological Movement in the World Today." 25.

Catholicism, created by the impact and work of leaders such as John Carroll. In America the scene was being set for both a deeper application of theology but also Mariology. John Carroll was appointed the first bishop and archbishop in Baltimore, Maryland. Carroll offered solid leadership to Catholics who were working out ways to function best in the new republic. Carroll's overall contributions were of great significance to American Catholicism. An example of one of Carroll's legacies is that he granted requests from Carmelite nuns to establish a foundation in the Baltimore diocese. "Soon after, the Sulpicians, also specifically devoted to Mary, established the first seminary in the United States, St. Mary's Seminary in Baltimore."[31] In 1833 the Sisters of Charity of the Blessed Virgin Mary, were established. Five young women from Ireland relocated to Philadelphia in order to teach the Indians about the faith. With the growing population in the United States, an American enthusiasm was becoming more evident. The many immigrants, along with further cultural developments in the late 19th century all contributed in spreading this American excitement that Catholic figures such as Cardinal James Gibbons and Archbishop John Ireland were able to capitalize on; "In 1913 the building of the national shrine of the Immaculate Conception on the campus of The Catholic University of America was suggested by Bishop Thomas J. Shahan, the university's fourth rector."[32] This religious growth was visible proof that the Catholic influence in the new world was here to stay. Along with the visible examples of the building of the national shrine, there was also an emphasis of Thomistic thinking being presented to seminarians and religious orders as

---

[31] Mary Christine Athens, "Mary in the American Catholic Church," *U.S. Catholic Historian*, Col. 8. No. 4, Bicentennial Symposium: Historians and Bishops in Dialogue (Fall, 1989), 107.

[32] Mary Christine Athens, "Mary in the American Catholic Church," 110.

initiated by Leo XIII and updated by Jacques Maritain and Etienne Gilson. This focus on Thomistic thinking would be something Carol would address in his Marian publications.

There were a number of themes, such as his Franciscan heritage, Scotistic and Thomistic research and even his research in Coredemption, that would shape Carol's theological environment. Again, Kozack, in her thesis entitled: "The Primacy of Christ as the Foundation of the Coredemption: The Mariology of Fr. Juniper B. Carol, O.F.M." (1911-1990), states: "The first overarching theological theme that shaped Carol's theological environment was ultramontanism. Although papal infallibility is limited to *ex cathedra* definitions, many Catholics, including theologians, took all of the Pope's theological statements as having extreme significance for determining the Church's teaching."[33] We of course value the teachings of the Church, specifically of the Pope, but many approaches to this fidelity to the Pope were distorted. For Carol, there was a genuine concern to keep a proper balance. Kozack continues, "Although not influenced by the political struggles that fed into the original growth of ultramontanism in Europe, ultramontanism still developed in America, albeit in a different form, which emphasized personal devotion to the papacy and upheld this loyalty to the pope as a means of establishing Catholic identity."[34] Carol would continue to uphold his loyalty and devotion to the pope in his writings and vocation.

---

[33] Kozack, *The Primacy of Christ as the Foundation of the Co-redemption*, 13.
[34] Kozack, *The Primacy of Christ as the Foundation of the Co-redemption*, 13.

1.8. The Mariological Context with regard to Carol's Lifetime

For Carol, his interest in Marian studies and priesthood started as a young boy and continued into his adulthood.[35] At the age of twenty-four (1935) we know Benjamin Carol was interested in studying more about the Mother of God and Soteriology.[36] This interest continues as we note that his doctoral work was on Coredemption, (*De Corredemptione Beatae Virginis Mariae*, (1950), with publications continuing in this area until 1978.[37] Because of his close collaboration and relationship with Father Carlo Balic, O.F.M., whom Carol considered to be one of the greatest scholars of the century,[38] it is probable that Carol's work about the *Debitum Peccati* was due in part to his translating work while at the Quaracchi.[39] The college of St. Bonaventure is located at Quaracchi, a Franciscan center of historical research and study.[40] Father Juniper describes Balic as a "towering figure," in Scotistic and Mariological studies in general. Carol writes, "My greatest indebtedness to Fr. Balic, is due to the tremendous assistance he gave me in my [M]ariological studies. As moderator of my doctoral dissertation, he was most generous with his time and advice—although he was also extremely demanding regarding scholarly precision. It was Fr. Balic who got me interested in the question of the so-called debitum peccati in Mariology, and he

---

[35] *The Provincial Annals*, Vol. 40, 1991 Pg. 109. Says, "He attended local schools but by the age of thirteen knew he wanted to be a priest."

[36] According to "Questionnaire for IV Year Theologians," Carol, when asked what he would like to write on said, "I have also a liking for writing along the line of Soteriological Mariology."

[37] See *Mary's Coredemption in a Petition of the Cuban Hierarchy to Pius XII*, Marianum 40 (1978), pp. 440–44.

[38] See Carol, "The Mariological Movement in the World Today." 38 (footnote 40.).

[39] *The Provincial Annals*, Vol. 40, 1991, Pg. 110.

[40] https://www.encyclopedia.com/religion/encyclopedias-almanacs-transcripts-and-maps/quaracchi As of 3/31/2019.

often encouraged me to continue his own anti-debitist crusade."[41] The indebtedness, to which Father Juniper refers, involved not only a scholarly method, and in part the selection of major areas of research such as the *debitum peccati*, but also the articulation of a vision of Mariology within which the particular specializations, both in regard to theme and argumentation, can be understood and assessed.

It is worth noting that Kozack looks at Carol's Mariology from the perspective of Vatican II. She writes, "Analyzing the Marian Pontifical publications during the years of Father Carol's writing and publishing efforts will assist us in laying an ecclesial foundation for our continued examination of Carol's mariological contribution."[42] As previously stated, it is not probable that Carol's Mariology was one that made a great contribution to any particular field that had not already been articulated. Carol's gift of consolidating and presenting the breadth of a particular Marian topic was exceptional. Kozack writes, "In his pre-Conciliar work, Carol argued that Mary immediately participated in the objective Redemption by co-meriting with Christ. His main argument in support of this position was based on the Patristic principle of recirculation-association and Mary's role as the New Eve. After the Second Vatican Council, Carol began to study topics related to the predestination of Christ and Mary."[43] Again, while we can agree with Kozack it is also noted that the topics studied and published are a synthesis of previous publications by Mariologists. This thesis is not stating that he did not lend an insight to Mariology; rather, that he gave the totality of an

---

[41] See Fehlner, "Fr. Juniper B. Carol, O.F.M.: *His Mariology and Scholarly Achievement."* 21.

[42] Kozack, *The Primacy of Christ as the Foundation of the Co-redemption*, iv.

[43] Kozack, *The Primacy of Christ as the Foundation of the Co-redemption*, iv.

argument with considerable fairness which certainly lends to thorough Mariological studies.

During Carol's life the Church will have a number of Mariological documents which will be noted here in this thesis in order to provide a Mariological context for Carol's publications. Carol was ordained in 1935, and so this thesis will look at Marian Magisterial publications after that time until his death in 1990. In some instances, we will see Carol's publications connect perfectly with what the Church is focusing on in Marian teaching, in other cases Carol may have little to say about what the Church is addressing and instead focuses on something else.

The first Marian Magisterial publication is *Deiparae Virginis Mariae*, an encyclical by Pope Pius XII, which was published on May 1, 1946, in order to explore the interest in the possible dogmatic proclamation of the Assumption of the Blessed Virgin Mary. From 1936 until 1948, Carol will publish 18 articles on Coredemption before presenting his first published work on the Assumption, entitled, "The Definability of Mary's Assumption," in the *American Ecclesiastical Review*. He will publish again with the same journal a year later in an article entitled, "Recent Literature on Mary's Assumption." We know that on November 1, 1950, the Apostolic Constitution *Munificentissimus Deus* dogmatically proclaimed the Assumption of the Blessed Mother. In the very first publication of *Marian Studies* released in March of 1950 (eight months before *Munificentissimus Deus*) Carol writes about the Assumption stating: "Our Lady's bodily Assumption, more than any other theological question, continues to engage the almost undivided attention of Catholic scholars everywhere."[44] Three

---

44 Carol, "The Mariological Movement in the World Today." 37.

more articles were published by Carol on the Assumption, all in 1951. The majority of his publications from 1936 to 1957's book *Mariology*, would be on Coredemption. He would include a chapter in 1957's second volume of *Mariology* entitled: "Mary's Death and Bodily Assumption," by Lawrence P. Everett, C.SS.R., S.T.D.[45] It must be noted that the theologians contributing to this three-volume work on Mariology are each in their own way valid scholars working independent of Carol's Marian emphasis, which seems to be more as a collector and gatherer of current Marian discussion publications and not so much a unique Mariological exploration and contribution. While it is realistic that Carol approved and included these works by various theologians in his comprehensive Marian publication, it is not necessarily true that Carol, nor any of the contributing authors, fully supported each person's Marian conclusions. What we can glean from this first comparison of Pope Pius XII's, *Deiparae Virginis Mariae* and Carol's publications, is that Coredemption was still at the heart of his publishing focus.

The second Ecclesial Marian publication occurs the following year, after *Munificentissimus Deus*, when Pope Pius XII promulgated, *Ingruentium Malorum* on September 15, 1951, emphasizing the importance of the recitation of the Rosary. In the third volume of *Mariology*, Father Carol includes a lengthy treatment on the Rosary by Msgr. George W. Shea, S.T.D.[46] I do not see any other publication, either personally or editorially from Carol on the Rosary.

---

[45] See Father Juniper B. Carol, O.F.M., *Mariology* 2, (Milwaukee, The Bruce Publishing Company, 1957), 461–492.

[46] See Father Juniper B. Carol, O.F.M., *Mariology* 3, (Milwaukee, The Bruce Publishing Company, 1961), 88–127.

Another important encyclical was promulgated on October 11, 1954, by Pope Pius XII. *Ad Caeli Reginam* which looks at the devotion to Mary as Queen. Carol does explore Mary's Queenship in his book, *Fundamentals of Mariology*, published in 1956.[47] In Father Carol's second volume of *Mariology* this topic is addressed at length in the chapter entitled, "The Universal Queenship of Mary" by Firimin M. Schmidt, O.F.M.Cap., S.T.D.[48] There are no other publications by Carol or edited by him on the topic of Queenship.

The encyclical of Pope John XXIII on the Rosary, *Grata Recordatio* on September 26, 1959, was soon followed by the very important eighth chapter of *Lumen Gentium* from the Second Vatican Council. Father Carol included in his second volume of *Mariology* a treatment on this chapter eight, by Cyril Vollert, S.J., S.T.D. entitled "Mary and the Church."[49]

Over the years this Ecclesial placement of Mary by the Popes within a theological framework for catechesis, culminated at the Second Vatican Council in the document *Lumen Gentium*. For some, the Second Vatican Council seemed to reorder the placement of Mariology solidly and fittingly within the context of the Church, and not as a field of study independently treated. Not everyone viewed it as advantageous. Tina Beatti, an English theologian and mariologist, in her article entitled "Mary Eve and the Church":

> Mary's place in relation to Christ and the church formed one of the most contentious issues of the Second Vatican Council. The so-called Marian

---

[47] See *Fundamentals of Mariology*, New York, Benziger, 1956, 72-86. (Henceforth cited as *Fundamentals*).

[48] See Carol, *Mariology* 2, 493–549.

[49] See Carol, *Mariology* 2, 550–595.

maximalists campaigned for a separate conciliar document devoted to Mary, while the so-called minimalists campaigned for her inclusion in the document on the church. In the end, the vote was 1,114 in favor of including her in the document on the church, and 1,074 against. As a result, Mary forms the subject of Chapter 8 of *Lumen Gentium*, a move which was intended to curtail the tendency to accord her a position of individual devotion outside the context of Christ and the church.[50]

With this ecclesial act, Chapter 8 of *Lumen Gentium*, many discerned incorrectly that Marian devotion was reserved for acts of piety and not for the Church at large. Mary Christine Athens also discusses the impact of Marian devotion post Vatican II when she writes:

> The question is often asked, how could all of the Marian devotions of the period before Vatican II have evaporated so quickly? The emphasis of the Council on Scripture and on liturgical renewal tended to put Mary into a new perspective. Rather than being downplayed, she was restored to her place as Mother of the Church. The last chapter of *Lumen Gentium*, where Mary is reflected on *within* the Church, is clearly one of the most important documents of Vatican II.[51]

---

[50] Tina Beatti, "Mary, Eve and the Church", *Maria* 2 (2001) 5–6. (This paper was originally given as the Marian Study Center Candlemas Lecture, at Ushaw College, Durham, on Monday 31 January 2000.

[51] Mary Christine Athens, "Mary in the American Catholic Church," 110.

For Athens, and many others, I am not sure they answer the question of why Marian devotions seem to evaporate, but it is clear that Pope John Paul II will bring a deeper devotion to Mary back through his actions and publications, all without disconnecting Mary with the Church. Kozack draws attention to the ecclesiotypical school and Christotypical school where she says:

> One common way of discussing the ecclesiotypical school and the Christotypical school is to call them the minimalists and the maximalists, respectively. These terms at first glance seem appropriate. The Christotypicalists were seeking new Marian dogmas, which can be considered an attempt to increase, or maximize, Mary's status with new definitions that would further highlight her unique role in the Church. In contrast, the ecclesiotypical school desired to emphasize Mary's membership in the Church, which could be seen as an attempt to decrease, or minimize, her status by highlighting how she is similar to other members of the Church. However, such terminology, and more importantly, such an understanding of the two schools, is problematic.[52]

This tension seems to be a matter of one's starting point, as Kozack concludes, "Both groups discussed Mary's relation to Christ and to the Church. The difference is one of starting point and emphasis, not of complete rejection."[53]

---

[52] Kozack, *The Primacy of Christ as the Foundation of the Co-redemption*, 49.
[53] Kozack, *The Primacy of Christ as the Foundation of the Co-redemption*, 50.

The fact that Father Carol was passionate about the truth and his devotion to the priesthood, the Marian movement and the Church, is noteworthy in a time of confusion concerning Mariological emphasis.

When it comes to Carol's publications after Vatican II, so much of them continued dealing with the Predestination of Mary, the *Debitum Peccati* and Coredemption.

On November 21, 1973, "Behold Your Mother" was published by the United States Conference of Catholic Bishops. There are no other publications from Carol that year except the report he published in *Marian Studies* 24, on the St. Louis Convention.

"On February 2, 1974, Pope Paul VI published an Apostolic Exhortation for the Right Ordering and Development of Devotion to the Blessed Virgin Mary, On February 2, 1974 a feast day which received a name change in the post-Vatican II liturgical reform and hence a shift from its connotation as a Marian feast day to a Christ-centered celebration Pope Paul VI chose to publish a Marian document for the right ordering and development of the devotion to the Blessed Virgin Mary."[54] *Marialis Cultus.* Pope Paul VI in *Marialis Cultus* presented this document not so much about Mary's person and role as such, but about the way the Church celebrates liturgies that commemorate Mary, her virginity, and about Marian devotion. *Marialis Cultus* is actually the practical application of the *Constitution on the Sacred Liturgy* on Marian devotion. The *Constitution* only has one reference on paragraph 103 and tells of the love of the Church.

---

[54] https://udayton.edu/imri/mary/m/magisterial-documents-marialis-cultus.php As of 3/25/2019.

"*Marialis Cultus* was influenced by the *Constitution on the Sacred Liturgy* from Vatican II, even though the Constitution has only one reference to Mary in paragraph 103. Article 103 tells of the *love* of the Church for Mary and the *inseparable bond* linking Mary to her son's saving work. These themes occur repeatedly in *Marialis Cultus*. The second major influence was *Lumen Gentium's* chapter 8."[55]

One of the great Marian Magisterial documents was released on March 25, 1987, entitled *Redemptoris Mater*, which explored the role of Mary in the economy of salvation. Carol published the year before, *Why Jesus Christ?*

On August 15, 1988 *Mulieris Dignitatem* was published by Pope John Paull II, discussing the dignity and vocation of women. This Apostolic Letter, published on the feast of the Assumption, looks at the nature between Mary and women.[56] There is nothing I have found published by Carol looking at the connection of Mary and femininity.

Before Carol's death in April of 1990, *Redemptoris Custos* was released on August 15, 1989, as an Apostolic Exhortation of John Paul II. Great interest in Marian studies will come back into the forefront because of St. John Paul II's love for Mary, which both found importance in the devotional and academic contributions of Marian studies.

The previous mentions of Marian publications simply provide a context in which we can see the areas of Mariology addressed by the Church during Carol's life. We note that there

---

[55] See, https://udayton.edu/imri/mary/m/magisterial-documents-mulieris-dignitatem.php As of 3/25/2019.

[56] See, https://udayton.edu/imri/mary/m/magisterial-documents-mulieris-dignitatem.php As of 3/25/2019.

was great interest by Carol in the person and work of the Blessed Mother, especially Coredemption. For Carol, this focus on Coredemption, the *Debitum Peccati*, and even the Predestination of Mary with her Son would occupy the majority of his publications throughout his life. Even after Vatican II his Mariology did not seem to deviate much from what his original interest was, from his formative years in seminary until his death in 1990.

1.9. Mariological Overview Specific to Carol

After looking at the general Mariology published by the Church during Carol's lifetime (1946-1989), we will now look at the Mariological overview specific to publications by Carol. The first Marian doctrinal writings we will examine, specifically by Father Carol, centers upon, Our Lady's predestined primacy with and under Jesus.[57] In this section our study will selectively[58] look at these primary texts since they best cover his perspective on this doctrine.

---

[57] Father Carol had a vast comprehension of the history of Mariology. A couple of Carol's book titles will exemplify his emphasis on Mary's predestined primacy with Christ, each filled with an extensive theological development and history of the subjects discussed: *The Absolute Primacy and Predestination of Jesus and His Virgin Mother*, Franciscan Herald Press, *Why Jesus Christ?*, Trinity Communications, *The Universal Primacy of Christ*, which Carol translated from the work of Francis Xavier Pancheri, O.F.M.Conv. Also, his 3-volume work, *Mariology*, by Bruce Publishing, which contains important insights not only from Carol but also many other Mariologists, which give a picture of Mariology during that time. In this thesis there are some footnotes and sentence structures that correspond to the website, www.amsterdamapparitions.com . Any connection to this site is due to an original paper by the author Chris Padgett from a directed study in 2005 with Dr. Mark Miravalle. This was not a professional publication, academic nor scholarly, and was originally placed on www.motherofallpeoples.com . Any reference to Juniper Carol matched within this thesis to either of these websites are in no way the property of any person, ministry or business except Chris Padgett. See also, pp. 23,25,26 and 88.

[58] These are chosen because they have the most comprehensive work concerning the primary points on this topic.

1979

"Reflections on the Problem of Mary's Preservative Redemption", *Marian Studies* 30 (1979): 19–88.

1980

"The Absolute Predestination of the Blessed Virgin Mary", *Marian Studies* 31 (1980): 172–238.

1981

The Absolute Primacy and Predestination of Jesus and His Virgin Mother, (Chicago, Franciscan Herald Press, 1981), xiii, 1–177.

1986

Why Jesus Christ? Thomistic, Scotistic and Conciliatory Perspectives, (Manassas, Virginia, Trinity Communications, 1986), xvii, 1–531.[59]

For Carol, the two primary methods of study in Our Lady's predestined primacy with and under Jesus are the Thomistic and Scotistic. In looking at these two methods, Kozack mentions Scotistic thought in her thesis on Carol. She writes:

> Christ's soul has the greatest glory; therefore, it should be willed not only before the rest of the predestined, but also before the permitting of the opposite of predestination, damnation. Following

---

[59] Concerning book, *Why Jesus Christ?*, Father Gambero puts this under 1985, but Fehlner under 1986. The actual publication date is 1986.

this logic, Scotus comes to his position on the relationship between the Fall and the Incarnation:

> If man had not sinned, of course, there would have been no need of a redemption. Still it does not seem to be solely because of the redemption that God predestined this soul to such glory, since the redemption or the glory of the souls to be redeemed is not comparable to the glory of the soul of Christ.[60]

There is something appealing about the Incarnation not being necessarily connected to the fall. Carol would highlight the Franciscan position in his publications but not without giving due diligence to the Thomistic thought. Kozack continues:

> Neither is it likely that the highest good in the whole of creation is somethings that merely chanced to take place, and that only because of some lesser good. Nor is it probable that God predestined Adam to such a good before he predestined Christ.

> To Scotus, it does not seem fitting that the Incarnation, the greatest act of God, should be conditioned not only on the existence of Adam, whose existence is a lesser good, but also on the Fall, which is an evil. Yet, if the "sole purpose" of the Incarnation was the Redemption, the Incarnation would have been willed for the lesser good of the restoration of the human race.[61]

---

[60]   Kozack, *The Primacy of Christ as the Foundation of the Co-redemption*, 5.
[61]   Kozack, *The Primacy of Christ as the Foundation of the Co-redemption*, 5.

In Carol's book, *Fundamentals of Mariology* (1956), he gave three propositions concerning the predestination of Mary but certainly leaned in favor of Scotus, and specifically the work done by Balic.[62] Concerning Carol's predisposition towards Scotus, Father Peter Fehlner wrote:

> We might say that Fr. Juniper's was an *anima naturaliter Franciscana*, a mind predisposed to admire and follow the great Franciscan masters, especially the Ven. John Duns Scotus, to appreciate the intimate connection between the subtle metaphysics of Scotus—revolving about the christocentrism of St. Francis (the primacy of Christ the King and conformity to Christ crucified) and Mariology in a Franciscan key (centered on the Immaculate Conception)—even if he was rather disinclined personally toward the intricacies of scotistic metaphysics.[63]

But Carol also makes sure to point to the opposing view when looking at Scotistic thought in Mary's universal predestination with her Son, which in this case was held by the Thomistic School.[64] Carol extensively goes through the Thomistic and Scotistic perspectives along with the many variables promoted by each of these schools of thought. Carol also investigates the predecessors who have published within this particular Marian field, placing his work on Mary's universal predestination within the context of Franciscan and Dominican fields of thought. In Carol's book, *The Absolute Primacy and Predestination of Jesus and His Virgin Mother,*

---

[62]   Carol, *Fundamentals*, see footnote 31., 21-25.

[63]   Peter D. Fehlner, O.F.M.Conv. "Fr. Juniper B. Carol, O.F.M.: His Mariology and Scholarly Achievement." *Marian Studies* 43 (1992): 18.

[64]   Carol, *Fundamentals*, 23, See footnote 32.

31

from as early as 659 with Isaac of Nineveh until William of Ware, O.F.M. (d. 1300), Scotistic predecessors are briefly examined. Father Carol is certainly aligned with a Scotistic school of thought, but he is careful to present adequately the Thomistic perspective.

> "During the course of the nineteenth century, as we pointed out, the doctrine of Mary's absolute predestination turned out to be one of the arguments frequently exploited by bishops and theologians in their letter to Pope Pius IX in favor of the Immaculate Conception. That the Pope himself incorporated this feature into his Apostolic Constitution *Ineffabilis Deus* seems rather obvious from some of the passages of that document."[65]

In his concluding remarks concerning Mary's predestination, Carol gives a synopsis of the perspective of Scotus and his followers stating, during the Pre-Scotus Period, there are seven Franciscans and eight others supporting the Franciscan perspective. In the 14th Century, there are eleven Franciscans with eight others; 15th Century, 12 and 12; in the 16th Century, 14 and 18; the 17th Century, 66 and 84; 18th Century, 18 and 27; 19th Century, 27 and 128; and in the 20th Century, 229 Franciscans and 211 others.[66] Five years later, in 1986 in his book, *Why Jesus Christ?* Father Carol expands his research offering a richer examination of the topic concerning Mary's predestination with her Son.

---

[65] Father Juniper B. Carol, O.F.M. *The Absolute Primacy and Predestination of Jesus and His Virgin Mother*, 147.

[66] See Carol, *The Absolute Primacy and Predestination of Jesus and His Virgin Mother*, 147.

This teaching of Marian predestination is of great importance, having noted the foundation for the dogmatic declaration of Mary as the Immaculate Conception. Having been intentionally selected as the Mother of God,[67] Mary, with Christ, was predestined by the will of God the Father, thereby giving back to the Trinity the greatest glory offered by humanity.[68] Applying the teaching of Mary's predestined primacy with and under Jesus to the redemptive aspects of the Incarnation will be later examined in order to clarify theological positions in Soteriology and Mariology. This association with her Son's salvific work is one that Carol explores repeatedly. According to, "Questionnaire for IV Year Theologians," when asked what he would like to write on Carol said, "I have also a liking for writing along the line of Soteriological Mariology."[69] His doctoral work is focused on Coredemption, as are the numerous publications in *Marian Studies*, magazines and books, such as *Fundamentals of Mariology*. Carol emphasizes in his publications from 1936 until 1985, the collaborative unity of mother and son in participating in the soteriological mission of Jesus.

The Second Vatican Council provided a clear foundation for Carol's Marian emphasis in the predestined Mary and Coredemption, when it stated:

---

[67] H.M. Manteau-Bonamy, O.P., *Immaculate Conception and the Holy Spirit: The Marian Teachings of Father Kolbe*, (NY, Prow Books/Franciscan Marytown Press, 1977), 5.
Bonamy, writes about St. Kolbe, a Polish Conventual Franciscan friar who looks at Our Lady's relationship with the Holy Spirit and her Immaculate Conception. "In the Holy Spirit's union with Mary we observe more than the love of two beings; in one there is all the love of the Blessed Trinity; in the other, all of creation's love.".

[68] This is differentiating Mary as a fully human person (one nature), from Jesus, who is One Divine Person with two natures: fully human and fully divine.

[69] "Questionnaire for IV Year Theologians," 1.

The Father of mercies willed that the Incarnation should be preceded by assent on the part of the predestined mother, so that just as a woman had a share in bringing about death, so also a woman should contribute to life. This is preeminently true of the Mother of Jesus, who gave to the world the Life that renews all things, and who was enriched by God with gifts appropriate to such a role.[70]

For Carol, Mary's association with Jesus is not dependent upon, nor impacted by, the stain from Adam, because Jesus' Incarnation was not reliant upon the first sin of Adam and Eve. His Incarnation and dwelling among us was the perfect expression of the Father's love toward His creation. Although Father Carol is a Franciscan, his scholarly work has been balanced in fairly presenting differing viewpoints.[71] The focus of Carol's publications remains on Mary with Christ in Mary's predestination with her Son, the *Debitum Pecatti*, and Coredemption, regardless of the school of thought.

The contribution of Carol's work, specifically Mary's predestined primacy with and under Jesus, while primarily Franciscan, is also fair in sharing various views different than his own. This doctrine of Mary's Predestination with her Son necessitates a deeper analysis of Mary's collaboration with her Son's salvific work as Coredemptrix. For Father Carol, his publications in Mary's predestination may be the fruit of his earlier work in which he looked at length into the controversy

---

[70] Austin Flannery, O.P., *Vatican Council II, Lumen Gentium, 56* (NY, Costello Publishing Company, Inc., 1975), 415.

[71] Examining the meticulous documentation in, *Why Jesus Christ?* is an example of the diligence in balanced scholastic presentation that Father Carol undertook in his writings.

over the *Debitum Peccati*. The matter of Mary being or not being the recipient of the debt of sin was primarily put to rest with the dogma of the Immaculate Conception, yet its theological controversy was an important topic for Father Carol, since it ultimately led to the dogmatic proclamation by the Church in 1854.

Another area of prominence in Mariological study for Father Carol is his penetration of the controversy[72] surrounding the *"debitum peccati."*[73] How is Mary to avoid the debt of sin common to all? Is her redemption unique, and if so, how can it be addressed? In the chapter discussing this doctrine our study will use these primary works, which highlight best Carol's understanding of this topic:

1956

Fundamentals of Mariology, New York, Benziger, 1956, pp. xx, 1–203.

---

[72] In a letter to Father Koehler on June 4, 1979 Carol says, "Maybe you have seen the review of my book on the debitum which appeared in *Ephemerides Mariologicae*. When I saw who the author of the review was, I knew what to expect. He (Father Fernandez) is the author of a book which tries to "prove" that the traditional teaching of the Church on original sin has to be totally revised. Adam and Eve never existed; original sin is only a myth; the teaching of St. Paul (Rom. 5) and the Council of Trent have been misunderstood for centuries; etc. etc. Naturally, if original sin does not exist, the question of the debitum becomes entirely meaningless. In this he is logical and consistent. But I prefer to follow the constant teaching of the Church and ignore all these new heresies. May God have mercy on our "expert" scholars!" 1. (This is from a letter found at the J.B.C. Memorial Library, Tampa, Florida. University of Dayton, International Marian Research Institute archives).

[73] "In general, the *debitum peccati* may be defined as 'the universal necessity to contract original sin.'" Father Juniper B. Carol, O.F.M., *A History of the Controversy Over the "Debitum Peccati."* in *Franciscan Institute Publications; Theology Series No. 9*, ed. George Marcil, O.F.M. (Bonaventure, NY, The Franciscan Institute of St. Bonaventure University, 1978), 4.

1977

"The Blessed Virgin and the "Debitum Peccati." A Bibliographical Conspectus", *Marian Studies* 28 (1977): 181–256.

1978

A History of the Controversy over the "debitum peccati", St. Bonaventure, New York, The Franciscan Institute, St. Bonaventure University, 1978, pp. xiii, 1–260.

Father Carol's book, *A History of the Controversy over the "Debitum Peccati,* gives the reader a careful analysis of the topic of the debt of sin, examining the period from the middle of the 12th century until 1977. Again, Father Carol is decidedly Franciscan in his approach, but he is careful to give the other perspectives a balanced presentation. In fact, he cites almost three hundred authors who are against his thesis.[74]

While the topic of Mary and the *Debitum Peccati* seems to be of little interest to Mariology in our time.,[75] Father Carol was interested in the Franciscan Mariological contribution of this topic, especially as it surrounded her Immaculate Conception. While we have moved away from many of the heated debates between the Franciscans and Thomists because of *Ineffabilis Deus*, Carol shows the Mariological progression of the *Debitum Peccati*, in his book, *A History of The Controversy Over The "Debitum Peccati"*, published in 1978. Because it

---

[74] See Father Juniper B. Carol O.F.M., *A History of the Controversy Over the "Debitum Peccati"* vi.

[75] On a personal note, I was told to avoid this topic of the *Debitum* by a known Mariologist, because of firstly, its surrounding controversy, and secondly, due to the fact that the matter had been settled with the dogmatic declaration of the Immaculate Conception.

was a big part of Father Carol's focus in his publications on Mariology, we will revisit this controversy in this thesis.

Original sin impacts all of humanity,[76] and its application to us as descendants of Adam brings about questions concerning Mary's preservation from it. What is Mary redeemed from if she is not found with sin? What type of redemption would she have? With the definition of Our Lady's Immaculate Conception in 1854,[77] we have clarity from a magisterial perspective concerning her singular and preservative redemption. One remaining question within Carol's Marian studies,[78] was whether Mary was ever, or could ever have been under the debt of original sin. How far does the reach of Adam extend to this daughter of Zion, who is understood to be completely separate from the stain of sin? While the topic is vast as to its history,[79] the answer is not.

The redemptive role of Christ is imperative to Father Carol's Trinitarian understanding of soteriology and theological expression, as demonstrated in his publications, and thus it has

---

[76] See Rom. 5:12.

[77] See *Ineffabilis Deus*.

[78] Carol writes in his book, *A History of the Controversy Over the "Debitum Peccati."* "The theological debate was partially settled by the dogmatic pronouncement embodied in the Papal Bull Ineffabilis Deus of 1854. Still some disputed aspects of the dogma concerning Mary's Immaculate Conception were untouched by the papal definition, thus leaving the matter open to further discussion by theologians. One of these disputed aspects concerns the so-called debitum peccati in Our Lady.", Father Juniper B. Carol, O.F.M., A History of the Controversy Over the "Debitum Peccati." in Franciscan Institute Publications; Theology Series No. 9, ed. George Marcil, O.F.M. (Bonaventure, NY, The Franciscan Institute of St. Bonaventure University, 1978). v. (prefatory note by John Cardinal Wright).

[79] Regarding the *debitum peccati*, Carol says, "To undertake even a superficial commentary on the immense bulk of texts we have been able to assemble during the past four decades, and to arrange the massive whole into a creditable synthesis, would require, besides two large volumes, many months of careful analysis," *A History of the controversy over the "Debitum Peccati,"* 3.

Mariological ramifications for Carol in that he sees Our Lady as Coredemptrix. In the chapter addressing this doctrine of Mary as Coredemptrix, this study will reference these primary sources:[80]

1936

"In Defense of the Title of Co-redemprix", *The Homiletic and Pastoral Review* 36 (1936), 1197–99.

1943

"Our Lady's Part in the Redemption According to Seventeenth-century writers", *Franciscan Studies* 24 (1943), 3–20; 143–58.

1956

Fundamentals of Mariology, New York, Benziger, (1956), xx–203.

1957

Mariology, ed. J. B. Carol O.F.M., vol. 2, (Milwaukee, Bruce Pub Co., 1957), xxii–606.

In examining a "Questionnaire for IV Year Theologians," which Carol filled out around 1935, we can see just how important Mariology is to Father Juniper. When asked what qualifications he has for teaching, he said, "During four years I have spent quite a bit of time in the study of Marian theology, especially the soteriological aspect of the 'Principis Consortii' which links the Blessed Virgin to Christ in His work

---

[80] As with the other Marian topics, these texts have the greatest amount of material on the subject matter being highlighted.

as Redeemer."[81] Her association with Jesus' redemptive mission as Coredemptrix is the final area of emphasis for our review concerning this Franciscan theologian's Marian focus. Coredemption was a very important topic for Carol, and when asked if he had an area of interest or any particular qualification for writing, he states: "I have also a liking for writing along the line of soteriological Mariology."[82] And again in the seventh question concerning specific learning or qualifications valuable to the Franciscan order or the Church, he simply writes, "Soteriological Mariology."[83] He would later emphasize in *Homiletic and Pastoral Review* that, "There are few doctrines in the vast field of Mariology which have enjoyed as much immunity from opposition as the doctrine which teaches that our Blessed Lady is a true, though secondary, co-factor in the Savior's redemptive work."[84] Coredemption is not a novel idea within the realm of theology during Carol's time, in fact, he states, "Actually, it can be traced back to at least the fourteenth century in a liturgical book preserved with other manuscripts at St. Peter's in Salzburg."[85] We will look at more of this in the specific chapter on Coredemption. In addition to the historical development of this doctrine by various theologians, the Second Vatican Council bespeaks this Marian teaching in *Lumen Gentium*, promulgated November 21, 1964:

> Thus the Blessed Virgin advanced in her pilgrimage of faith and faithfully persevered in her union with her Son unto the cross, where she stood, in keeping with the divine plan, enduring

---

[81] Juniper, B. Carol, O.F.M., "Questionnaire For IV Year Theologians", (1935), 1.

[82] Carol, "Questionnaire For IV Year Theologians", 1.

[83] Carol, "Questionnaire For IV Year Theologians", 1.

[84] Father Juniper B. Carol, O.F.M., "In defense of the title of co-redemptrix" *The Homiletics and Pastoral Review,* 36 (New York, NY, 1936), 1107.

[85] Carol, "Our Lady's Coredemption", *Mariology* 2, 422–23.

with her only begotten Son the intensity of his suffering, associated herself with his sacrifice in her mother's heart, and lovingly consenting to the immolation of this victim which was born of her. Finally, she was given by the same Christ Jesus dying on the cross as a mother to his disciple, with these words: "Woman, behold thy son" (Jn. 19:26-27).[86]

Carol did not publish anything about the Marian work of Vatican II. His focus seems to be on the primacy and predestination of Jesus and Mary.[87]

1.10. Contribution

Father Carol and other theologians contributed much to further clarify Marian doctrines such as Coredemption, the primacy of Mary with Jesus and related aspects. As we will see, especially in matters of Mary's Coredemption, some of the difficulties with this teaching lean more towards an ecumenical sensitivity to the title than a negation of the teaching itself.

In 1955 Rev. Cyril Vollert, S.J., President of The Mariological Society of America, wrote concerning Father Juniper Carol O.F.M.: "He is unquestionably the most prominent Mariologist in the United States and ranks with the best in the world."[88] In 1991, when Father James McCurry, O.F.M.Conv. penned his homage to Father Carol in the 42nd edition of *Marian Studies*, he stated: "Fr. Juniper, a simple friar,

---

[86]   Flannery, O.P., *Vatican Council II, Lumen Gentium, 58* (NY, Costello Publishing Company, Inc., 1975), 417.

[87]   See, 1981's, *The Absolute Primacy and Predestination of Jesus and His Virgin Mother,* and *Why Jesus Christ?* 1986.

[88]   Juniper B. Carol, O.F.M., pref. note, Rev. Cyril Vollert, S.J., *Fundamentals of Mariology*, (New York, Benziger Brothers, Inc. 1956), x.

common fellow, whom some might have regarded this side of eternity as a 'diamond in the rough,' was and ever will remain for this Society that reveres him an "immortal diamond."[89] Father Juniper Carol's mariological contribution can be seen from his numerous publications to lectures and Marian movements. In 1956 Carol published, *Fundamentals of Mariology* contributed to Marian theology in that he focused on the mission and prerogatives of Mary. The former does in fact explore the primary topics we have discussed, such as the Predestination of Mary and Coredemption, but it also looks at Mary's Spiritual Motherhood, her dispensing of all graces, and her Universal Queenship.[90] The latter, looks at her Immaculate Conception, Immunity from Actual Sin her death and Assumption.[91] Carol has left an outstanding legacy of veneration to Mary, if not because of a new way of understanding Mary, most certainly due to his organizational contribution to the field of Marian studies.

---

[89]   James McCurry, O.F.M.Conv. "Fr. Juniper B. Carol, O.F.M., 1911–1990: Vir Catholicus Et Totus Apostolicus." *Marian Studies* 42 (1991): 14. (from now on notated as, McCurry, "Fr. Juniper B. Carol, O.F.M., 1911–1990.").

[90] See *Fundamentals*, 21-86.

[91] See *Fundamentals*, 87-199.

A Biography of Father Juniper B. Carol, O.F.M.

The life of father Juniper B. Carol, O.F.M., from his early years in Cuba and brief education at Tusculum College (High School) in Greenville, Tennessee to his spiritual formation in Havana and entrance into the Franciscans at the Holy Name Province in New York, was both typical and atypical. This study will also include information about his education overseas, teaching and pastoral commitments, as well as his work establishing and maintaining a Mariological contribution with publications and the founding and participation in the Mariological Society of America. This biography will do two things: first, it will flesh out the context of his life, and second, it will emphasize some of the reasons Father Carol's Marian "synthesis"[92] is of importance.

1.11. The Early Years

Father Juniper B. Carol, O.F.M., was born in Cardenas, Cuba, on February 19, 1911, and was the youngest of Cyprian (Cipriano Carol y Sicard)[93] and Aquirregaviria Carol's eight children. Cyprian was born in Matanzas, Cuba. The Carol family brought the child to the sacrament of initiation and, "He was baptized under the name Benjamin."[94] His baptism date was August 29th, 1911, with the services held at La Purisima

---

[92] See McCurry, "Fr. Juniper B. Carol, O.F.M., 1911–1990," 12–13.

[93] This Information on Father Juniper Carol was given to me in printed form by Father Dominic Monti, O.F.M. It is from the personnel files of the Holy Name Province, Order of Friars Minor. 3.

[94] Theodore A. Koehler, S.M., "In Homage to the Founder of the Mariological Society of America Juniper Benjamin Carol., O.F.M. (1911–1990)." *Ephemerides Mariologiae*, Annus LIII-Fasc.II-n.142, (Rome, 1991), 709.

Concepcion[95] by the Reverend Venancio Novo.[96] Little is known about the Carol family during Benjamin's early years. There was Benjamin's sister Maria Josefa (the mother of Father Carmel Lluria, Juniper's nephew), his brothers Luis, Jose M., and Albert J. Albert was born in 1898 in Cuba and eventually moved to Florida before his death 1985. We also know of a nephew, John J. O'Higgins Jr.[97] In my email correspondence with Father Peter Fehlner, F.I., he related historical information concerning Carol's family, which he personally gathered at an unspecified time from the Franciscan friar. Father Fehlner states:

> (Benjamin Carol's) mother's family was Spanish in origin and closely related to the Cardinal Archbishop of Havana, who died just as Castro took power at the end of 1958. His father's family had emigrated from Ireland sometime during the 19th century. Carol is a Hispanic corruption of the family name, in Ireland commonly spelled Carrol or O'Carroll. The family certainly belonged to the upper classes in Cuba. Perhaps the English family: Carroll, some of whose members were early Catholic settlers of Maryland and in the subsequent history of the Catholic Church in the USA, and in England prominent supporters of the Catholic Church, is related to the Irish clan, or what seems the Anglo-Irish clan. Fr. Juniper called my attention

---

95 The accents common to the Spanish language will not be utilized within this thesis since it does not change the meaning of the word with their absence.

96 This Information on Father Juniper Carol given to me in printed form February of 2013 by Father Dominic Monti, O.F.M. It is from the personnel files of the Holy Name Province, Order of Friars Minor. 2.

97 See, Father Dominic Monti, O.F.M. It is from the personnel files of the Holy Name Province, Order of Friars Minor, 2.

to the fact that three priests in some way connect to this Irish clan and as Mariologists were contemporaries: Fr. Michael O'Carrol, a Holy Ghost priest in Dublin, Fr. Eamon Carrol, O. Carm., and Fr. Juniper Carol, OFM.[98]

Benjamin Carol's godfather was the future Cardinal, His Eminence, Manuel Arteaga y Betancourt, Archbishop of Havana. This Archbishop of Havana, Cardinal of the Church, would be involved in many of Carol's important religious moments, even at Carol's ordination many years later. "Cardinal Arteaga preached at Fr. Juniper's first Mass."[99] Carol's father was a successful merchant[100] and a strong Catholic in Cardenas. Cyprian would have known many in Church leadership, so the relationship Juniper's father Cyprian developed with Cardinal Betancourt is understandable.

The Carol family was not only invested in the children's spiritual formation, but also their children's academic development, as we will see when Benjamin and some of his siblings travel to the United States for schooling. Cardenas, the city in which the Carol's lived, was certainly less developed than Havana, yet advanced in soap and cotton factories, breweries, and distilleries. Concerning this city, Jose De Olivares in 1899 writes: "The city of Cardenas, situated thirty miles distant from Matanzas, is perhaps the one striking example of modern progressiveness to be found in all the island

---

98 This information comes from email correspondence with Father Peter Fehlner on 2/5/2013 who stated that he learned this in a "brief and very superficial conversation with Fr. Juniper."

99 "Cardinals Have Siena Friends," *The Siena News: Newspaper of America's Youngest College*, 7. No. 9. February 28, 1946., 1.

100 Cyprian was the head of a lumber company according to the Matriculation Blank filled out by Casto Carol Aquirregaviria for Tusculum College on Sept. 11, 1923.

of Cuba."[101] Descriptions of Cardenas speak of its heat, flat terrain, and the constant barrage of mosquitoes

1.12. Religious Training

From the age of thirteen, Benjamin Carol began to discern a vocation to the priesthood.[102] Before entering the diocesan minor seminary in Havana, Carol spent a year of high school at Tusculum College in Greenville, TN, in 1923. This brief time at Tusculum College is worth considering further. In 1923, at the age of twelve, Benjamin Carol and several of his siblings journeyed to Tennessee in order to attend school.

Discerning how the Carol children found themselves in East Tennessee at a decidedly Presbyterian College was a mystery. Kathy Cuff heads the archives department at Tusculum College and found relevant information concerning Carol in the college's archives.

Tusculum Academy was founded in 1795 by Samuel Witherspoon Doak. It was originally used as a high school, since there was already a College in the Greenville, Tennessee area. He was a Presbyterian minister and insisted that each President of his institution be a clergy member as well. Samuel Doak also stated that if at any time there were more than three professors employed at Tusculum, two-thirds of them had to be of the Presbyterian denomination. From 1908 until 1932, Charles Oliver Gray was the president of Tusculum College and a Presbyterian minister, according to Doak's stipulations. President Charles Gray's administrative position would coincide

---

[101] Jose De Olivares, *Our Islands and Their People as seen with Camera and Pencil*, (St. Louis, New York, Chicago and Atlanta, Introduced by Major-General Joseph Wheeler. N.D. Thompson Publishing Company, 1899), 149.

[102] See "Fr. Juniper Carol," *The Provincial Annals,* (staff writer) 40, 1991, 109.

during the time of Benjamin Carol's enrollment. Also during this time, the college employed a beloved professor, Landon Carter Haynes. Daddy Haynes, as he was affectionately called, taught for 68 years at Tusculum and was known to have had a great love for the Spanish language. Landon would ask students to teach him Spanish whenever opportunity presented itself.

Landon Haynes and many citizens in East Tennessee "became involved in the Spanish American War in 1898, largely because there were a number of volunteers from the area. On commencement day at Tusculum, there was a tension in the air because of the uncertainty of developments in Cuba."[103] Grace Haynes, in the book *The Daddy Haynes Story, the Life of Professor Landon Crater Haynes*, also mentioned that "Daddy" Haynes went on a trip to Cuba in 1906, 1907. This may have been the time when Carol's family could have been introduced to Tusculum College.

> At the time that Professor Haynes visited Cuba, an interest in schools was being left there. In Cardenas, some 75 miles east of Havana, the Presbyterian Church U.S.A. had lately started a mission school, which later grew into a flourishing institution, La Progressiva Presbyterian College.[104]

In 1923, Tusculum College had in its "Register of Students"[105] record of Father Carol and his brothers Casto, Luis

---

[103] Grace Haynes, *The Daddy Haynes Story, The Life of Professor Landon Carter Haynes*. (Morrison Printing CO. Charlotte, NC, 1968), 127.

[104] Grace Haynes, *The Daddy Haynes Story*, 160–161. This time would have been around 1906–1907 according to pg.159.

[105] *One Hundred And Thirtieth Year, Tusculum College, Annual Catalogue, 1923-1924 With Announcements for 1924-1925*, (Greenville, TN, Published by Tusculum College, May, 1924), 74. (Forthwith abbreviated as *Tusculum*, pg.).

and Edward in attendance. Casto Carol was in the "Third Year," Luis Carol in the "Second Year,"[106] and Benjamin and Edward in the "First Year."[107] The expense of this school at the time the Carol children attended was twenty dollars for 12–16 credits, with other expenses such as room and board and laboratory fees. "All bills for each semester are to be paid in two installments, one-half at the beginning and one-half at the middle of the semester."[108] Benjamin's father must have made quite a decent salary to afford this educational opportunity for his children, unless special financial scholarships were extended to them.

Benjamin Carol's educational stay in the United States is known from the information found on the admission form for Tusculum College in Tennessee. While at Tusculum College, Benjamin was accompanied by his siblings Luis, Edward and Casto. From the information given in the matriculation blank forms, an application sheet asking pertinent questions concerning areas of academic interest, it can be deduced that Luis J. Carol, born in Cardenas on August. 24, 1904 (seven years older than Benjamin), Edward and Casto Carol Aguirregaviria were together with Benjamin for that academic year in Tennessee. It is unclear as to whether the parents accompanied them to the United States of America, but the trip itself would have been lengthy by ship and train. According to the matriculation form, Benjamin's brother Casto wanted to be a Civil Engineer, at least in September of 1923, and their parents were listed on the forms as being merchants. Cipriano, the father, was the head of a lumber company, according to Casto's

---

[106] *Tusculum*, 73.

[107] *Tusculum*, 74

[108] *Tusculum*, 86.

school form, even supplying the address for the entire Carol family at that time: Apartment 228 in Cardenas, Cuba.

In 1924, Tusculum College closed its high school department so that the college could receive accreditation, resulting in the construction of the Chuckey-Doak High School. This meant that the young Carols would not be able to continue the following year within the same academic institution, and as a result, Benjamin Carol and his siblings left Tusculum College and returned to Havana, Cuba.

Having returned to Cuba, Carol journeyed to Havana and entered the diocesan minor seminary of St. Charles, studying there from 1924 until 1930.[109] This training would have included the basics of education equivalent to a high school curriculum, with a preparatory formation in philosophy and religious studies to get students ready for major seminary.[110] In the early years of his minor seminary studies at the age of thirteen, Benjamin Carol was confirmed on December 5th, 1925, at the Chapel of the Archbishops.[111]

His mother had a great love for the Franciscans, especially St. Francis, and this devotion of hers would be the catalyst for his interest in the Franciscans, Order of Friars Minor. Benjamin would make his way back to the United States

---

[109] See Theodore A. Koehler, S.M., "In Homage to the Founder of the Mariological Society of America Juniper Benjamin Carol., O.F.M. (1911–1990)." *Ephemerides Mariologiae*, Annus LIII-Fasc.II-n.142, (Rome, 1991), 707–22.

[110] I have been unable to receive Carol's transcripts from the minor seminary in Cuba and will not speculate on what specific courses he took during those years.

[111] See Father Dominic Monti, O.F.M. It is from the personnel files of the Holy Name Province, Order of Friars Minor. 2. This Information on Father Juniper Carol was given to me in printed form.

in order to join the Franciscans, having connected with an American couple who visited the Carol family while in Cuba.[112]

On August 20, 1930, Carol began his novitiate in Paterson, New Jersey, to become a Franciscan in the Holy Name Province. He then received the new name Juniper. Following his simple profession on August 24, 1931, he began theological studies at Holy Name College in Washington, D.C.[113]

The provincial minister for the Franciscans during the time Carol entered the novitiate was Father Mathias Faust. Father Faust would hold this position for four terms the years of 1919–1925 and 1931–1937, "then as custos (1937–1942), before appointment as the Order's general delegate for the Americas (1942–1947), and general procurator (1947–1951)."[114] This period for the Franciscans in Paterson was one of great growth of which Father Faust was very much a part. The life of a novitiate was not an easy one and Carol published nothing about this time of training. To determine what Father Carol's life was like in the early years of his novitiate and religious life we can look at the account of Father James Schuck, who was received into the novitiate just a few years after Carol (Carol in 1930 and Schuck in 1933). Father Schuck eventually became a bishop on February 24, 1959. He was appointed by Pope John XXIII, and was consecrated in Holy Cross Cathedral, Boston, as titular bishop of Avissa and prelate nullius of Christalandia, Brazil.[115] White quotes Schuck who gives an

---

[112] See, "Father Juniper Carol," (*The Provincial Annals*, 40, 199, New York, NY, Holy Name Province), 109.

[113] Koehler, "In Homage to the Founder of the Mariological Society of America," 709.

[114] White, *Peace and Good in America*, 133.

[115] https://hnp.org/who-we-are/our-friars/deceased-friars/james-d-schuck/

example of the novitiate that reflects what it would have been like for Carol:

> I can't forget the 4:40 rising, the coronas
> [rosaries], the endless public prayers, the playing
> of handball and tennis in habits and sandals, the
> sparse meals, the infinite peeling of potatoes in
> the dank cellar room, the grim soul-searching
> under the long shadow of the master...I now
> realize the purpose of the strictness of our novice
> master, Fr. Jerome Dawson: to cut us down to
> size—the size of a Friar Minor. But I must admit
> that the cutting-down process was painful to
> take.[116]

This novice master Father Jerome, appointed in 1922, in his obituary was described as "a strict disciplinarian who demanded undeviating regularity and obedience to the minutest points...He would tolerate no half-measures in any of his novices."[117]

Because Benjamin Carol had previous education in Havana, he did not attend St. Joseph Seraphic Seminary at Callicoon, New York. Father Dominic Monti, O.F.M., who has been the Provincial Vicar of Holy Name Province since 2005, told me in a phone call in February of 2013 that St. Joseph Seraphic Seminary was a 'minor seminary'—4 years of high school and the first 2 years of college. There was no postulant year at that time for clerical candidates, a term used by Father Monti for those interested in priesthood. Upon completing their studies in Callicoon they entered the novitiate directly. Typically, the men were about 20 years old. After the novitiate,

---

[116] White, *Peace and Good in America*, 136–37.
[117] White, *Peace and Good in America*, 137.

as temporary professed clerical brothers, they completed their philosophical studies in Croghan, NY and Butler, NJ receiving a BA from St. Bonaventure University. The Callicoon, Croghan, and Butler programs were accredited through Saint Bonaventure University.[118]

In a phone interview with Father Dominic Monti O.F.M. on February 4, 2013, Monti mentioned that Father Carol's not attending St. Joseph Seraphic Seminary might have been a disadvantage for him. Most of the men entering the Franciscan order were just finishing up their 8th grade of schooling or joined right after high school. These young men would spend time at Callicoon bonding. They would have taken the usual courses in math and science, but also an intense emphasis was placed on languages to prepare them for future theology and philosophy courses.[119] When Carol arrived in Paterson, New Jersey as a novitiate in 1930, he was already at a disadvantage, not necessarily because of his age or academic preparation, but because he had not had the chance to build relationships with the other students who were already well bonded. Father Monti described novices this way:

> Novices were formally received at a public ceremony in August. To the ritual question "What, my dear son, do you request?" Each replied, "Reverend Father, I ask you, for the love of God, of the ever-blessed Virgin Mary, and of our holy Father Francis and of all the saints, to give me the habit of the Seraphic Order, that I may do penance, amend my life, and serve God

---

[118] From an email dated February 26, 2014. If you want more from Father Monti see Appendix C.

[119] See White, *Peace and Good in America*, 135.

faithfully until death. After removing his coat
and tie, the novice was clothed with the habit.
The celebrant announced, "In the future you will
be called Frater___(Juniper)___" often the name
of a Franciscan saint.[120]

After his novitiate, Father Carol would go to Washington, D.C.
in 1931 for four years of study at the Holy Name College.
Father Mathias Faust received his solemn vows on September
17,1934. He was ordained upon completion of the ordinary
theological courses at Holy Name College. [121] Carol's
ordination was on February 20, 1935 at the Immaculate
Conception Shrine in Washington, D.C.[122] Bishop James Ryan
was presiding.

According to the Fiedsam Memorial Library Archives,
from the Summer of 1934 until 1937, Father Juniper Carol was
the Assistant Professor of Modern Languages, specifically
Spanish at St. Bonaventure College in Bonaventure, NY,
meaning he would teach the students Spanish whenever the
school needed. This academic institution would garner some
notoriety having employed Thomas Merton in the early 1940's
as the Assistant Professor of English.[123] While Father Carol was
no longer at the university when Merton arrived, it is clear that
the latter was not a great fan of the friars. Joseph W. White
wrote the history of the Holy Name Province and had this to say

---

[120] White, *Peace and Good in America*, 225.

[121] See "Rev. Fr. Juniper Carol, O.F.M. Was Rewarded", *The Provincial Annals* 8 No. 3, (1950), 50. As a small side note, this Annal has Carol's ordination on Feb. 20, 1945, which is at odds with other published *The Provincial Annals* 17 (1960), 121.

[122] See, Koehler, "In Homage to the Founder of the Mariological Society of America," 709.

[123] See Friedsam Memorial Library Archives Biographical Pages.

about Thomas Merton's pointed observations about how the friars lived at St. Bonaventure's (1940-41):

> If the Franciscans in this country stuck to their rule and didn't have so many dispensations, so many radios, such taste for golf and creature comforts—if they were tonsured, and said Office in Choir more, and knew something about the Liturgy and about singing and about poverty, it would be a fine Order. But they are all fine fellows. It is just that this country has ruined their rule for them.[124]

Father Juniper, in 1934-1935, "was assigned to the faculty of St. Bonaventure College. A year later (1936, CP) he was permitted to do research work in his favorite subject, Mariology, at the College of St. Bonaventure, Quaracchi, near Florence, Italy."[125] The place of study in Quaracchi, Italy was the respected Franciscan "center of medieval research and publications"[126] and would be very important for Carol and the future Mariological Society of America. "As early as 1936 he had written "Our Lady's Co-Redemption Vindicated" while at Quaracchi."[127] Father Carol continued to work with ancient manuscripts. He loved his Mariological studies, but he did not particularly enjoy this tedious assignment of working on the critical edition of Scotus in Florence. The Provincial of the Franciscans at the time of Father Carol's passing was Father Flavian Walsh, O.F.M. He wrote a letter to those within the

---

[124] White, *Peace and Good in America,* 190–191.

[125] *The Provincial Annals* 6, (New York, NY, Holy Name Province ,1947–1948), 301.

[126] Koehler, "In Homage to the Founder of the Mariological Society of America," 709

[127] Flavian A. Walsh, O.F.M. Provincial Vicar, (Holy Name Province, April 9,1990): Letter of Father Carol's passing, 1.

order discussing Carol's time in Italy. Walsh said that Father Carol found the work laborious and very unpleasant. He states:

> (Juniper) sailed for Italy where he began his life of theological endeavors. From 1936 to 1937 he was in Quaracchi—a year which he found "unbearable" as he spent "five to six hours every day behind ancient manuscripts with a microscope in my hand trying to decipher hieroglyphics." Juniper then moved on to the Pontifical Athenaeum of St. Anthony's in Rome where he pursued his theological studies from 1937 until 1940 when he received his Doctorate of Sacred Theology.[128]

Theodore Koehler, S.M writes about Carol's studies, "From 1937 to 1940, he pursued his theological studies at the Pontifical Athenaeum of St. Anthony in Rome and prepared a doctoral dissertation on Mary's co-redemption."[129]

Carol finished his doctoral work in 1940 but was forced to return to the United States before his defense, due to World War II. "I left Italy on June 2," stated Fr. Juniper. "If I had been allowed to remain about two weeks more, I would have received my degree."[130]

---

[128] Flavian A. Walsh O.F.M. Provincial Vicar, (Holy Name Province, April 9,1990): Letter of Father Carol's passing. 1. This publication states Carol's STD is complete in 1940, yet the war hinders his defense, which would be accepted in 1950.

[129] Koehler, "In Homage to the Founder of the Mariological Society of America," 710.

[130] "Skull-Cap of Pius XII Prided Possession of Fr. Juniper," *The Siena News: Newspaper of America's Youngest College*, 3. No. 5. Loudonville, NY. October 25, 1940., 1.

Father Carol had as his mentor and doctoral advisor Father Balic who would become a "life-long friend."[131] In a 1992 account of Father Carol's Mariology Father Fehlner wrote the following in *Marian Studies* concerning Carol's advisor:

Father Juniper describes him as a "towering figure," not only in scotistic and mariological studies in general, but in his own life as well. "My greatest indebtedness to Fr. Balic"—he writes "is due to the tremendous assistance he gave me in my mariological studies. As moderator of my doctoral dissertation, he was most generous with his time and advice, although he was also extremely demanding regarding scholarly precision. It was Fr. Balic who got me interested in the question of the so-called debitum peccati in Mariology, and he often encouraged me to continue his own anti-debitist crusade." The indebtedness to which Fr. Juniper refers involved not only scholarly method and in part selection of major areas of research, but also the articulation of a vision of Mariology within which the particular specializations, both in regard to theme and argumentation, can be understood and assessed.[132]

Not only was Carol working on his "doctoral dissertation on Mary's co-redemption"[133] at the Pontifical

---

[131] Peter D. Fehlner, O.F.M.Conv. "Fr. Juniper B. Carol, O.F.M.: *His Mariology and Scholarly Achievement." Marian Studies* 43 (1992): 21.

[132] Fehlner, "Fr. Juniper B. Carol, O.F.M.: *His Mariology and Scholarly Achievement."* 21.

[133] Koehler, "In Homage to the Founder of the Mariological Society of America," 710.

Athenaeum of St. Anthony's in Rome, but he spent some time exploring Mariology and considering ways to convey teachings on Mary to those speaking English. This consideration may have aided in establishing the Mariological Society of America. He asserted the following from an editorial perspective:

> The definite need of a comprehensive symposium, in the vernacular, covering the entire theological tract relative to Our Blessed Lady. As a result of those preliminary deliberations, the editor undertook to elaborate a suitable program to meet this deficiency as far as the English-speaking public was concerned.[134]

Due to the World at War, Carol knew that dreams of establishing a symposium on Mary would be put on hold until further notice. Carol continues:

> While the global conflagration which followed in 1939 virtually shattered any hopes of immediate action in this respect, nevertheless the original idea continued its process of development during the war years until it reached the desired maturity. The establishment of the Mariological Society of America in 1949 may be credited with having contributed considerably toward carrying the original plans into effect.[135]

Those original plans of meeting the need of a comprehensive symposium to English speaking people that covered the entire

---

[134] Fr. Juniper B. Carol, *Mariology* 1, (Milwaukee, The Bruce Publishing Company, 1954), ix.

[135] Fr. Juniper B. Carol, *Mariology* 1, (Milwaukee, The Bruce Publishing Company, 1954), ix.

theological tract relative to Mary may have had some difficulties being brought about in the late thirties, but ten years later those plans began to take shape.

1.13. A World at War: Teaching in the States

As mentioned, Father Carol was forced to leave Italy when the war sent him stateside. During this time in America, Carol began to teach at Siena College in Loudonville, NY, in 1940, and continued to teach there as needed until 1948. In addition to teaching, Carol along with other priests from the College preached at various churches during the Jubilee year as per the instructions of his Excellency, Most Rev. Edmund F. Gibbons, bishop of Albany, NY. This was "an effort to stimulate interest in the Propagation of the Faith," in 1940 and was held at St. Patrick's, in Watervliet, NY.[136] Father Carol's teaching responsibilities at Siena College was languages, music, and theology. While at Siena, as reported by the staff writers at *The Siena News*, he also organized the Siena Opera Forum, and in order to promote the opera "founded the Music Forum. Father has taught Spanish, Italian, Apologetics, Literature, and History of Opera."[137] "Fr. Juniper, in speaking of the year's activities in the Forum, expressed pleasure at 'the favor with which we were always welcomed,' and hoped that the next years activities would be as successful."[138] Really, the school appreciated Carol's contribution to their music program. *The Siena News* wrote, "This forum, by the way, has been weaned and diapered by the Reverend Juniper B. Carol, O.F.M., and from all

---

[136] "Faculty Members Aid in Jubilee Drive," *The Siena News: Newspaper of America's Youngest College*, 3. No. 4. Oct. 18,1940., 4.

[137] "Rev. Fr. Juniper Carol, O.F.M. Was Rewarded." (*The Provincial Annals*. Vol. 8 (New York, NY, Holy Name Province, 1950) n. 3), 50.

[138] "Forum Presents Spring Musical," *The Siena News: Newspaper of America's Youngest College*, 3. No. 5. May 2, 1947., 4.

indications it will blossom into the series of fine achievements still latent in the mind of its energetic creator."[139]

After teaching from 1940 until 1948 at Siena, and with things calming down a bit in Europe, Carol was given permission to finish his studies in Rome.[140] The departure from Siena to Rome necessitated some position adjustments, specifically in the Opera Forum. Before he departed, *The Siena News* reports that Carol "was guest of honor at a farewell party held on September 21. At the gathering, held at Catholic Union Hall in Albany, Fr. Juniper was praised for his fine efforts as Forum moderator and was presented a purse in appreciation."[141] How much money was presented in this purse is unknown. This Opera Forum provided the community an opportunity to hear some notable stars, such "as Vincenzina Franchini, grand opera soprano, and Jan Peerce, one of the foremost tenors in the nation, to Albany."[142] Much of the success of this Opera Forum was attributed to the efforts of Carol while there.

Siena College had a number of articles about Father Carol in their publication, *The Siena News.* One such article discussed Father Carol's visit with the Pope while he was in Rome during his studies. This meeting with the Holy Father was of great importance for the College, with *The Siena News* reporting the following:

---

[139] "Opera Forum Sponsors Grand Opera Concert," *The Siena News: Newspaper of America's Youngest College*, 7, No. 2. October 29, 1945., 3.

[140] See, *The Provincial Annals*, "Another Friar Named to Marian Commission," Vol. 6 (1947-48),302.

[141] "Forum Rule Changes Hands," *The Siena News: Newspaper of America's Youngest College*, 9. No. 2. October 8, 1947., 4. The purse is a certain amount of money. Amount is unknown.

[142] "Student Senate Enters New Field; Sponsors Concert," *The Siena News: Newspaper of America's Youngest College*, 10, No. 5. October 22, 1948.

On January 20, 1940, Father Juniper had a private audience with Pope Pius XII, at which time he received from the Supreme Pontiff a skull-cap worn by the present Pope. Although the friar had been privileged to see the Holy Father on a previous occasion, when he accompanied a Bishop to the Vatican, he was desirous of having a private audience. This was finally arranged through the Cuban Minister. He presented to the Holy Father a book which he had written on the Blessed Virgin Mary as the Co-Redemptrix of the human race. When the audience was over, the Holy Father asked the friar if he wanted any favor. Father Juniper requested the *pileolus* the Pontiff was then wearing, giving him a new one in exchange. The friar has treasured this keepsake ever since.[143]

In his own words Carol states:

After I was announced to the Holy Father, I entered the room in which he was seated. The Pope motioned for his secretary to leave and I was alone with the Head of the Church. Although I did not expect the Pope to be too austere, I, nevertheless, was surprised at his frank cordiality. We spoke Italian. I presented the Holy Father with a book which I had written, "Our Lady's Coredemption." He turned the pages of the book, passively, until he came to the chapter title: Pope Pius XII on the Coredemption. He

---

[143] *The Provincial Annals*, "Another Friar Named to Marian Commission," Vol. 6 (1947-48), 302.

said that he remembered when he had preached
on the subject in Lourdes. He also told me that
this was the room in which Pope Pius IX and
Pope Leo XIII died: Pius IX proclaimed the
doctrine of the Immaculate Conception and Leo
XIII wrote much on the Blessed Mother.[144]

The article from *The Siena News* continues:

Fr. Juniper stated that he could easily see the
Pope has been under great strain. The war has
upset the Holy Father greatly. He remarked that
the Holy Father was an excellent listener,
inspiring confidence and that he showed an avid
interest in his conversation. 'When I was about to
leave, the Holy Father asked me if I wanted
anything as a remembrance of my audience. I
replied that I would like a skull-cap The Holy
Father offered to get me a new one, but I asked
him if I might have the one he was wearing. He
replied by taking off the white skull-cap and
handing it to me.' The skull-cap now rests in a
bell-jar in Fr. Juniper's room and is one of his
most treasured possessions.[145]

One final note concerning Siena College, before Carol
left for his doctoral defense, while teaching at Siena College
Father Carol traveled to Spain. Flavian Walsh writes, "In 1947
he was invited to present his theological conclusions on "Mary's
Co-Redemption" at the Marian Congress held in Madrid,

---

[144] "Skull-Cap of Pius XII Prided Possession of Fr. Juniper," *The Siena News:
Newspaper of America's Youngest College*, 3. No. 5. October 25, 1940., 1.

[145] "Skull-Cap of Pius XII Prided Possession of Fr. Juniper," *The Siena News:
Newspaper of America's Youngest College,* 1.

Spain."[146] This opportunity to present to those in Spain about Mary as Coredemptrix was an honor for the college and the Franciscan community. From there Carol soon went to Rome. While Carol was at the Antonianum, the Pontifical University of St. Anthony in Rome, he was named to the Marian Commission, which was dealing with the future dogma of the Assumption. *The Provincial Annals* report that Father Juniper,

> A friar of Holy Name Province, who is at present attached to the Pontifical University of St. Anthony, Rome, was appointed Secretary General for the United States of the International Franciscan Commission of Mariology. The nomination of Father Juniper to this post was made on his feast day, January 4, by the Very Rev. Father Mathias Faust, Procurator General of the Order, who was acting General at the time.[147]

In 1949 Carol would make his defense for his doctorate. He then was able to publish his doctorate entitled *De Co-Redemptione B.V. Mariae* in 1950.

Father Koehler, S.M. recounts this period of Father Carol's defense in his published homage to the founder of the Mariological Society in 1991's *Marianum Ephemerides Mariologiae*.

> At last, in 1949, he returned to the Antonianum in Rome and was finally able to defend his doctoral thesis. As he explains in the preface to

---

[146] Flavian A. Walsh, O.F.M. (Provincial Vicar, Holy Name Province, April 9,1990): Letter of Father Carol's passing, 1.

[147] *The Provincial Annals*, "Another Friar Named to Marian Commission," Vol. 6 (1947-48), 301.

his book on Our Lady's co-redemption, he had planned, already in 1931, to present a thesis gathering all the documentation concerning this question in the theological tradition up to the present day. But for the defense itself of his doctoral work, it was soon apparent that he could present only one period: the seventeenth century.[148]

After the defense of his dissertation under the direction of Fr. Charles Balic, the rest of Carol's work was fully published in 1950 by the "Vatican Press as a substantial 639-page volume."[149] This written work was too lengthy for his oral defense. The defended portion was just a part of his entire project, "dealing with co-redemption as expounded by seventeenth-century theologians,"[150]

> In 1950, he published his complete work, *De Corredemptione Beatae Virginis Mariae. Disquisitio positiva.* He had consulted some 3,000 writers (see his preface). His bibliography contains 821 titles of books or articles written by some 559 authors who directly studied the question. The index goes further: 1,322 names (including 9 titles). His conclusion remained prudent; he favored the concept of the immediate cooperation of Mary in the work of her Son, our

---

[148] Koehler, "In Homage to the Founder of the Mariological Society of America," 710.

[149] Fehlner, "Fr. Juniper B. Carol, O.F.M.: *His Mariology and Scholarly Achievement.*" 19.

[150] Koehler, "In Homage to the Founder of the Mariological Society of America," 710.

Redeemer, but he acknowledged the opposition encountered by this option.[151]

This would become an important time for Carol, not only for the occasion of defending his doctoral thesis,[152] but also because he would see the beginnings of the Mariological Society of America. Father Walsh recounts the following about this period in Father Carol's life in his 1990 letter informing friars about the passing of Carol:

> In 1949 Juniper was the leading founder of The Mariological Society of America which he and a group of priests established in Washington, D.C. He became editor of "Marian Studies" which served to foster both devotion to and continued theological reflection on the theology of Mary. Juniper edited a three-volume work on Mariology which consumed much of his time between 1955-1961. In 1956 he also published "Fundamentals of Mariology." Fluent in Spanish, English, French, Italian and German, Juniper published over fifty articles in U.S and European scholarly journals.[153]

Having completed his studies and moving forward with more publications, Carol would also spend time teaching students. It was expected that education would serve a purpose

---

[151] Koehler, "In Homage to the Founder of the Mariological Society of America," 710.

[152] Which was held on June 26, 1948, *"and was approved magna cum laude."* Peter D. Fehlner, O.F.M.Conv., "Fr. Juniper B. Carol, O.F.M.: *His Mariology and Scholarly Achievement." Marian Studies* 43 (1992), 19., see footnote 3. See *Antonianum* 24 (1949), 145.

[153] Flavian A. Walsh, O.F.M. Provincial Vicar, (Holy Name Province, April 9,1990): Letter of Father Carol's passing, 1.

for the Franciscan community, specifically to aid in the formation of their own. According to Joseph White's book on the history of the Holy Name Province, there was an expectation for the friar to further their education and teach after ordination. He says, "From the 1940's, newly ordained friar-priests were expected to earn a master's degree—a program that they usually started in summer sessions between the academic years' theology studies. Many were prepared to teach soon after ordination. That teaching was part of their vocation was simply assumed."[154] In addition to the expectations of highly educated friars teaching fellow Franciscans, the necessity for quality publications was of increased importance to the Order. Joseph M. White writes, "In modern academic life, however, teaching alone was not enough. Publication of original research was increasingly expected of most college-level teachers—often as a condition of promotion and tenure."[155] The expectation for friars to teach and publish was considered so important that Father Thomas, gives a heated complaint about the lack of research coming from their writers and in 1950:

> I have something against you Doctors, Masters,
> and other people who could or should wield a
> facile pen. In spite of our numbers, we have but a
> measly corps of writers. As a result, the
> Franciscan Message resembles the feeble
> warblings of a solitary finch in the grove or the
> weak chirpings of a lonely sparrow on the
> house-top. Witness how other Orders are making
> their voices articulate in every department: the
> press, the radio, the forum. At the Council of
> Trent some seventy scholarly Friars walked into

---

[154] White, *Peace and Good in America*, 262.

[155] White, *Peace and Good in America*, 262.

the arena to propound and defend the teaching of Holy Church. If there were a Council today, maybe a Friar would be summoned to light the candles at the altar or carry the maniple for some Bishop from New Zealand.

Do not tell me that you have no time. Look at the voluminous writings of St. Anthony, St. Bernardine, and all the Franciscan Masters. They were busier than you or me, but they had the spirit and the will... Your Master's or Doctor's dissertation accorded you the license to teach and to write, not necessarily a free ticket to the golf course or other equally fruitless diversions. A teacher who from day-to-day does not progress in knowledge and research and who repeats his lessons in parrot-like fashion year after year is burying his five talents and is not paying back the Order what he owes...

We now have sixteen young men engaged in higher studies at various universities, and I am giving them fair warning that that Province expects more of them than just a high-sounding title and a skimpy thesis. What we want is a dedication to a career of research and a reasonable amount of class work to boot.[156]

Clearly Father Juniper was publishing regularly at this point, and nobody could rightly call his doctoral work simply high-sounding and skimpy. While Father Thomas' expectations for his friars may seem unrealistic to many, one thing is known

---

[156] White, *Peace and Good in America*, 262.

from White's *Peace and Good in America, A History of Holy Name Province Order of Friars Minor 1850s To the Present*, and that is,

> Some very bright friars had been assigned to earn doctorates, with or without interest in teaching. Once having achieved their degrees, they were not personally motivated to pursue further research and writing in their assigned field. Others, having earned a master's degree as expected, showed even less desire to teach, and without doctoral degrees, most were not adequately trained for scholarship. Many friars saw teaching primarily as an opportunity to engage in pastoral ministry to students, in which they were highly effective.[157]

We have seen that Father Carol not only received his required priestly education but also a Pontifical doctorate.[158] He taught in various institutions, such as St. Bonaventure, Siena College and Holy Name College, but not with the regularity that others with his credentials would have been expected to do. With that much training and expertise, the Franciscans would

---

[157] White, *Peace and Good in America*, 262.

[158] It is worth noting that achieving a Pontifical degree was different during Carol's time. Father Peter Fehlner says, "In those days there was no thesis required for the STL, other than the so-called written essay similar to the written exercises (exercitationes) required for major courses. For the STL far more important and more difficult even than the doctoral dissertation was the one hour oral exam before a board of four professors on the whole of theology (known as the exam on the 100 theses), each with 15 minutes to question the candidate: two professors for dogmatic theology, one for moral and one for Scripture. Before the reform of studies of Pius XI in 1932 (*Deus scientiarum Dominus*) this was the only requirement for the doctorate. After the reform the exam was required for the licentiate, whereas the dissertation was required for the doctorate. Anyone who did not do well (barely passed) in the oral exam could give up hope of being admitted to the doctoral program." From an email to Chris Padgett 9/27/13.

have had him teaching their friars at their academic institutions full time. Father Carol did in fact regularly publish and was certainly interested in extensive research (look at his bibliographies at the end of this thesis, and Mariological collection), so it is a bit of a mystery as to why he would not have been a regular educator up until his later years; he was academically and educationally what the Franciscans were looking for.

In 1952 and the following years, Father Carol would return to St. Bonaventure and give Mariological lectures during the summers. This was not a permanent position since he was residing primarily at Holy Cross in the Bronx from 1950-1956, but his presentations were of such interest to students that the content was regularly taught, and later gathered together and published as, *Fundamentals of Mariology* in March of 1956.

> (His classes were) attended normally by graduate students of the Department of Sacred Sciences, mostly sisters, and a few priests and seminarians. The publication of these lectures in book-form is intended to serve primarily as a textbook for seminaries and similar institutions for religious, although it is likewise suitable for instructing the laity, and even for supplying a theological basis to our Marian preaching.[159]

For Father Juniper, teaching and residing with the friars at St. Bonaventure and Siena College would have provided him with strong and vibrant Franciscan communities. There are a few things worth mentioning in connection with my interview with Father Dominic Monti. According to Father Monti, after

---

[159] Carol, *Fundamentals*, ix.

Carol received his doctorate, it was unprecedented that Father Carol did not begin working full time for the two growing Franciscan facilities that would train their friars, Holy Name College and St. Bonaventure University. Christ the King seminary would regularly have need of friars who had completed higher education. That much academic training given to a friar necessitated it being used to further educate the Franciscans. That Father Carol is given an opportunity as a friar at Holy Cross in the Bronx to do Mariological research full time is quite unusual. Father Monti simply can see no logical reason for Carol not to be "teaching our guys" and couldn't think of a single friar who would ever be a full-time writer. Father Dominic said that when he spoke to the three older priests that knew Father Carol, the exact phrase by all three was this: "he was a real character." Father Dominic said that he has been a Franciscan long enough to know that when that phrase is used it is often not an endearing one. His conclusion was either that Father Juniper was not really that good in the classroom, that he was disorganized, or that he was possibly some eccentric personality who did not necessarily gel with the Franciscan order in molding the minds of the young friars in the classroom.[160]

1.14. Carol's Marian Emphasis[161]

Carol lived his life advancing the universal primacy of Christ and worked to bring about a greater Marian devotion.[162] Through lectures, books, and numerous articles, Father Carol

---

[160] Interview with Father Dominic Monti, O.F.M. and Chris Padgett on 2/4/2013.

[161] The emphasis is within the context of Carol's publications in the three areas of Mariology I'll be emphasizing in the coming chapters.

[162] See McCurry, who says, "Fr. Junipers substance—his intellectual priorities and apostolate—was securely focused on one goal above all: the Primacy of Jesus Christ." James McCurry, O.F.M.Conv. "Fr. Juniper B. Carol, O.F.M., 1911–1990, *Vir Catholicus Et Totus Apostolicus." Marian Studies* 42 (1991): 11.

challenged minimalist and poor approaches in Mariology in the hopes that followers of Christ would honor Mary. Father James McCurry O.F.M. Conv. reflects on how Carol addressed incorrect teachings:

> Vigilant against such abuses, Juniper would be quick to write letters to various editors. He criticized the writer of a Letter to the Editor in a 1983 issue of the Homiletic and Pastoral Review. Citing the flawed letter, Juniper declaimed:
>
> He writes: "The Incarnation is not a necessity of the Divine Essence as Scotus maintains." Why no reference? Because none exists! The accusation is simply monstrous and incredible. Scotus happens to be the theologian who most vigorously stressed the freedom of God's will (In Metaphys. IX, 15; Coll. 16, n. 8).[163]

This compulsion to write and promulgate the truths of Mary, for Carol, was greatly enhanced because of the support of his religious superiors in allowing him such liberty as a friar.[164]

Mariology for Carol started with the Christological or Trinitarian perspective, and from this foundation a proper ecclesial understanding was established. How God considered and honored Our Lady, inasmuch as we can deduce this from Carol's publications, specifically *Fundamentals*, should impact our Marian expression. Father Carol writes:

> Because of her central position in the plan of God, the study of her mission and privileges will

---

[163] McCurry, "Fr. Juniper B. Carol, O.F.M., 1911–1990.," 13.

[164] See Carol, *Mariology* 2, viii.

necessarily widen and deepen our understanding
and appreciation of the various other phases of
Catholic theology. In a very true sense,
Mariology is like a compendium of all other
Christian dogmas.[165]

Having started the Mariological Society of America in
1949, which published the periodical *Marian Studies*, Father
Carol offered readers the opportunity to read about Mariological
issues both current and traditional. In addition to the publication
of *Marian Studies*, an annual symposium would highlight
certain Marian topics, inviting leading theologians to present
lectures and engage in further Mariological dialogue.[166] Father
Carol seemed to have a few Mariological topics he focused
upon, such as Mary's Predestination with her Son,
Coredemption, and the controversy surrounding the *"Debitum
Peccati."*. Concerning the Predestination of Mary with her Son,
Father Flavian Walsh writes:

Heavily influenced by the teachings of Duns
Scotus, Juniper was also a strong advocate of the
Queenship of Mary, and thus sharer in Christ's
dominion over all creation. Juniper further
clarified his theological reflections in 1981 when
he published 'The Absolute Primacy and

---

[165] Carol, *Fundamentals*, 3.

[166] In the bibliography I have made reference to *Marian Studies*, where Father Carol,
as editor of the periodical, and secretary for the Society, documented the topics
covered by varying theologians at each annual gathering. Topical examples are,
Our Lady and St. Paul's Doctrine on Justification, Our Lady and the Law of Sin,
(Vol.16). *Mary's Present Role in the Communion of Saints*, (Vol. 18), *Mary and
the Crisis of Faith*. (Vol. 20), etc.

Predestination of Jesus and His Virgin
Mother.'[167]

The second topic of Carol's interest dealt with the
controversy over the *"Debitum Peccati"*. This was a recurring
theme in his publications, where he provided extensive
bibliographies from varying positions on that particular topic.

The third topic Carol focused on concerned Mary's
Coredemption, Father Koehler, S.M. writes:

> Although the coredemption of Mary remained
> his main research interest, he published various
> studies on other Marian topics, in particular, the
> Immaculate Conception, the debitum peccati, and
> the Scotist teaching on the absolute primacy and
> predestination of Jesus and his Virgin Mother.[168]

Carol's love for publications centered on the
Coredemption was noted by Anna Wirtz Domas, in her book,
Mary USA. When considering the great contribution of Carol's
Mariological library Anna Wirtz Domas writes:

> An important Marian library was begun by
> Juniper B. Carol, O.F.M., at the Franciscan
> monastery in New York City. The collection
> comprised over twelve thousand items (books,
> pamphlets, articles) including photostatic copies
> and microfilms of hundreds of out-of-print
> pieces. It is estimated that Father Carol has
> virtually everything written on the co-redemption

---

[167] Flavian A. Walsh, O.F.M. Provincial Vicar, (Holy Name Province, April 9,1990):
Letter of Father Carol's passing, 1.

[168] Koehler, "In Homage to the Founder of the Mariological Society of America,"
711.

in any language. The collection has recently been divided, half housed in Tampa, Florida, the other half in Washington, D.C.[169]

1.15. The later years (1956-1990)

From 1956-67 Carol's official residence was at St. Bonaventure in Paterson, NJ. but he principally resided with the Missionary Sisters. In 1958, Father Carol became the chaplain for the Missionary Sisters of the Immaculate Conception in Paterson, NJ. He also taught them at Tombrock College. Two of these Missionary Sisters were given the opportunity to share memories of their teacher and chaplain Father Juniper Carol.[170] Their reflections offer a little glimpse into the life of Father Carol as priest and teacher, but the passage of time had diminished many of their recollections to a few examples. One thing common in their accounts was that Father Carol had a flair for the dramatic in the classroom.

Father Carol would have been attached to the local friar house, Holy Cross Friary, as would any Franciscan if they spent time teaching and doing missions around the areas of New Jersey and New York, but Carol was not regularly there. To Father Dominic Monti, O.F.M., it again seemed a bit odd that while Father Carol is teaching the Sisters, he primarily took up residence with them while providing pastoral service instead of the normal practice of going out from the friary.

In 1956–57 the Holy Cross Friary was a big house in Paterson called a mission band. Father Monti said that at any

---

[169] Domas, *Mary USA*, 273.
[170] See Appendix B for more of the interview done on 12/11/2012.

given time 15 to 20 Franciscans were assigned full time there, using it as a base while they were constantly on the move.

Eventually Father Carol would leave the Missionary Sisters, and Tombrock College would close. Ilene Greenfield Lumpkin writes, "The Garret Mountain Campus of Berkeley College was the former home of Tombrock College, which was run by the Missionary Sisters of the Immaculate Conception. Some of the nuns still lived on campus when Berkeley re-located there from East Orange in 1976."[171]

While Carol was known for his Mariological publications and teaching, he was also willing to help out in devotional works as well. One example thereof would be the translation of the Family Prayer Card. In order to aid families in prayer the Redemptorists created the Family Prayer Card in 1962 according to *The Siena News*.[172] When the Family Prayer Card was being translated into French, Carol made it available in Spanish, which was approved by the Most Rev. S. M. Metzger of El Paso, Texas, who said, "Over fifty thousand copies of the Spanish edition have been distributed by the Redemptorist Fathers in Puerto Rico alone."[173] Carol's contribution seems to be primarily in translation with no other major involvement.

Around the time of the Family Prayer Card the Catholic Church was clarifying her role in the world at the Second Vatican Council. The Council's announcement was January 25,

---

[171] Ilene Greenfield Lumpkin, "Berkeley College Honors Missionary Sisters of the Immaculate Conception at 75th Anniversary Celebration." September 27, 2006. (Berkeley College, 2007), 3.

[172] See, "French Family Prayer Card Available," *The Siena News: Newspaper of America's Youngest College*, 24, No. 13 Dec. 14, 1962., 4.

[173] "French Family Prayer Card Available," *The Siena News: Newspaper of America's Youngest College*, 24, No. 13 Dec. 14, 1962., 4.

1959, with the first session beginning October 11, 1962, and the fourth ending December 8, 1965. A great deal of debate would surround the Marian teaching during this Council. I asked Father Fehlner to speak a bit more about Carol's connection with Father Balic, who was Carol's mentor and doctoral director, and who was also present at Vatican II. He said this about their relationship:

> Fr. Juniper told me once that Fr. Balic had three Marian causes to promote: the definition of the Assumption, the definition of Marian mediation and coredemption, and the rebuttal of the *debitis* hypothesis in the Immaculate Conception. Fr. Juniper was assigned to work for the co-redemption cause and the eventual definition of that mystery (and late in life he took over the anti-debitist cause, still a hot issue). Initially, he once told me, he was to concentrate on speculate questions, but after a year (Fr. Juniper did not feel he was particularly gifted to handle scotistic metaphysics) he was assigned to concentrate on historical research, e.g., as in his doctoral dissertation. His Mariological manual is scotistic in orientation, yet the outline is essentially that of Fr. Roschini, not exactly a friend of Scotus. Yet Fr. Juniper was always on good terms with Fr. Roschini. As to Fr. Juniper's relations with Fr. Balic and the latter's role in Vatican II, I know from what Fr. Juniper told me that he was in continual contact by letter with Fr. Balic,

during and long after the Council was over, about what was going on.[174]

The contribution to Mariology from the Second Vatican Council's *Lumen Gentium* in its eighth chapter was rich in its content. While there were concerns during the Council of where the Marian treatment was to be placed, either in a document of its own or part of another, the need to speak about Mary was not in debate. Referring to the eighth chapter of Vatican II's *Lumen Gentium* the teaching on Mary is rich and beautiful.

> But it strongly urges theologians and preachers of the word of God to be careful to refrain as much from all false exaggeration as from too summary an attitude in considering the special dignity of the Mother of God. Following the study of Sacred Scripture, the Fathers, the doctors and liturgy of the Church, and under the guidance of the Church's magisterium, let them rightly illustrate the duties and privileges of the Blessed Virgin which always refer to Christ, the source of all truth, sanctity, and devotion. Let them carefully refrain from whatever might by word or deed lead the separated brethren or any others whatsoever into error about the true doctrine of the Church. Let the faithful remember moreover that true devotion consists neither in sterile or transitory affection, nor in a certain vain credulity, but proceeds from true faith, by which we are led to recognize the excellence of the Mother of God, and we are moved to a filial

---

[174] Email with Father Fehlner F.I., on 2/5/2013.

77

love towards our mother and to the imitation of her virtues.[175]

We do not have much from Father Carol about Vatican II. According to the publications from him on Mariology his views seemed unchanged, at least in the emphasis of publications before and after the Council.[176]

In 1967, Father Carol leaves Tombrock College and travels south to participate in various ministries as chaplain. This is another example showing how Father Carol seemed to find himself more and more disconnected from community life, which, as we have noted by Fr. Monti, was an oddity to all those in leadership positions within the Franciscans.

Father Carol moved down to Florida, certainly with permission, and was involved in a number of parishes. Flavian A. Walsh, O.F.M. writes:

> In 1979 Juniper retired to St. Anthony Friary in St. Petersburg, Florida after ten years serving as a chaplain in the Tampa, Florida area. Juniper enjoyed relatively good health until his surgery earlier this year. During the January provincial retreat, I spoke to him for over an hour in his

---

[175] *Lumen Gentium*, 67, 422.

[176] We will note this more in the coming chapters, but an example is: The primary works of predestination and preservative redemption are: *Fundamentals of Mariology*, New York, Benziger, 1956, pp. xx–203. "Reflections on the Problem of Mary's Preservative Redemption", *Marian Studies* 30 (1979), 19–88. "The Absolute Predestination of the Blessed Virgin Mary" *Marian Studies* 31 (1980), 172–238.
The Absolute Primacy and Predestination of Jesus and His Virgin Mother, (Chicago, Franciscan Herald Press, 1981), xiii–177., and *Why Jesus Christ?* Thomistic, Scotistic and Conciliatory Perspectives, (Manassas, Virginia, Trinity Communications, 1986), xvii–531. The primary ideas and presentations do not change from before to after Vatican II.

room when it was decided he should go to Ringwood for a month or two. His spirits were excellent and, although he feared flying, he agreed to go until he regained his strength and was able to care for himself again. His stay in Ringwood was brief, but he relished the constant care and atmosphere provided by Fr. Francis Soucy, his nephew Fr. Carmel Lluria, and the staff and friars. His final days were happy and peaceful.[177]

This time, from 1967–79, Father Carol spent time in Florida and time in New York. The time spent in Florida is quite unprecedented according to Father Dominic Monti's account. Maybe the difficulty Carol was experiencing within his community, as implied by Monti, had to do with Carol's outspoken opposition to Kennedy. Possibly, it could have been pressure from Cardinal Spellman to the Holy Name Province to find a way to remove Father Carol from the immediate area. Father Monti is quick to note that allowing Carol more space may have been a mutual benefit to both Carol and his order.

Father Carol was chaplain at St. Joseph's hospital in Tampa, Florida from 1967–68, so really, during those years in the Sunshine State, Carol was very much on his own.[178] It is likely that Juniper lived in the chaplain quarters for St. Joseph's hospital and not able to live in community, since there was not a friary in Tampa.

From 1968–69, Carol is a resident at St. Bonaventure at Paterson, but then moves back to Florida where he would once

[177] Flavian A. Walsh, O.F.M. Provincial Vicar, (Holy Name Province, April 9,1990): Letter of Father Carol's passing, 2.
[178] See, *The Provincial Annals*, "Fr. Juniper Carol," Vol. 40,1991. 109-112.

again be living alone. During this time, he is a Chaplain at St. Joseph's Hospital in Port Charlotte for four years, two years at St. Joseph's Manor in St. Petersburg, and three years at Cor Jesu Convalescent Center in Tampa.[179] Father Carol settles at Christ the King rectory in Tampa, Florida.

It wasn't until 1979 to 1990 that Father Carol would come to live in St. Petersburg, Florida, at the Franciscan retirement facility, finally living in community with other religious. From the year 1956 until 1979, Father Carol spent most of his life living in solitude. From Father Dominic Monti's perspective as an elder Franciscan, he has noticed over the years that some friars would perpetuate and cultivate the image of being a little odd, because they knew that people would not call upon them to do certain things." Father Monti thought it was possible that since Carol loved doing his Marian work, chaplaincy and publishing, that he may have really enjoyed his freedom. Father Monti also shared that it is true that there were certain locations to which priests would be sent if the friars in leadership were not sure about what place would be most ideal for their *unique* priests. It was also the case that if a particular friar was strongly opposed to the perceived liberal leanings of the Franciscans at the time, they would not allow them to form the minds of the incoming friars. Holy Cross in the Bronx was one such place that friars who didn't fit in would be sent; apparently Florida may have been as well.

What I begin to deduce from these documented and personal accounts is a picture of Father Carol, who while being very conservative in his theology, may have been at odds, according to Father Fehlner and Monti's suppositions, with the Franciscans willingness to tolerate certain liberal trends. We

---

[179] See, *The Provincial Annals*, "Fr. Juniper Carol," Vol. 40,1991. 109-112.

have hints of this when Carol openly speaks out against Kennedy and his lukewarm Catholicism, with his unwillingness to concelebrate, which may just be his preference, and even his tendency to be alone. Even Juniper Carol's association with The Mariological Society of America would diminish over the years, possibly against his wishes. Father Peter Fehlner recalls this about Fr. Juniper's removal as secretary of the Mariological Society (and the person with effective control over it) in the late 70's:

> At that time, I was a member of the Board of Directors of the Society and had a front seat view of ecclesiastical politics in action. A powerful group of the members led by Fr. Eamon Carrol wanted Fr. Juniper to retire because he was blocking a wider opening of the Society to theologians with rather modernistic views of Mariology, whereas Fr. Juniper insisted on fidelity to tradition as a condition for membership and for delivering conferences. Other reasons were given to the public to explain the "promotion" of Fr. Juniper to the post of President emeritus for life, but the one I just mentioned was the key motive, with implications that were this not done, then a great many members would drop membership. This group evidently got the ear of the Provincial of Holy Name Province (Alban McGuire, then a supporter of the more liberally orientated friars in control of the Province) and he ordered Fr. Juniper to step down as Secretary and accept the honorary title. Fr. Juniper obeyed without complaining or even comment, but I have often

suspected that he may have been deeply hurt not
only by the lack of support from his Province,
but also by the obedience to retire given him and
by the subsequent direction taken by the Society
founded by him.[180]

Whether others on the board or even within the Holy
Name Province saw it in this same way could be disputed, but
nonetheless, Father Carol was a man who likely had difficulty
playing politics and worrying about being a people pleaser. In
many ways this probably was a quality that both served him
well and created difficulties others would not appreciate. In a
letter written June 24,1976 to Father George F. McLean, O.M.I.
the secretary of JCCLS (Joint Committee of Catholic Learned
Societies and Scholars), at Catholic University of America,
Carol states:

> Personally, I cannot but applaud the willingness
> of American scholars to place themselves at the
> service of the Hierarchy if and when the latter
> asks for their scholarly opinions. But I most
> strongly disagree with the ideas which some of
> these scholars are trying to sell our Bishops, as
> well as with the questionable methods sometimes
> used to implement their "service" to the
> Magisterium. When I see the chaotic condition to
> which our so-called scholars have brought the
> world of theology, I cannot but thank God that
> He entrusted the teaching authority of His

---

[180] Peter Fehlner, F.I. email correspondence with Chris Padgett. 2/5/2013.

Church to the Pope and the Bishops, and NOT to our theology 'experts.'[181]

The work of Father Juniper Carol is primarily remembered within the realm of his publications in *Marian Studies*, as well as his Marian books, and the occasional times he was chaplain and professor. He continued to publish in Mariology even after leaving the primary secretarial responsibilities at the Mariological Society of America. These publications were not created to be another devotional expression of Mariology, rather, they were meant "to expound and elucidate the prerogatives of the Mother of God in a scientific manner,"[182] and his work was continued by publishing in other journals, magazines, and books.

Father Koehler notes the following:

From 1980 on, Juniper devoted his writings to the doctrine of Duns Scotus and the Scotist teachings on the primacy of Jesus and Mary. Juniper's last published writing—a 531-page book—was dedicated to that study: *Why Jesus Christ? Thomistic, Scotistic and Conciliatory Perspectives* (1986).[183]

Carol's love for learning and promotion of Marian studies is also demonstrated in his donation of books addressing numerous Marian topics to the library of the Franciscan Institute

---

181 Fr. Juniper B. Carol, O.F.M. Secretary of Mariological Society of America June 24, 1976. This letter was copied to Fr. Jelly, O.P. and sent out from Tampa, Florida.

182 Carol, "The Mariological Movement in the World Today." *Marian Studies* (1950): 25.

183 Koehler, "In Homage to the Founder of the Mariological Society of America," 712.

in 1984.[184] Having taught at Bonaventure University, and the various works being done at the school, Carol not only left a legacy of lectures students cherished and the reading public enjoyed from his publication of those summer course lectures of which *Fundamentals of Mariology* was a tangible fruit,[185] but also the gift of many of his Marian books to the library is still treasured there.

1.16. Carol's death and some remembrances

Father Carol passed away in 1990. Father Walsh, Provincial Vicar wrote concerning the passing of the friar:

> On April 1, at about 11:00 P.M. Fr. Juniper Carol died at Holy Name Friary in Ringwood, NJ. He had asked to go to Ringwood for post-operative care and some physical therapy after surgery at St. Anthony's hospital in St Petersburg, Florida, in January and was preparing to return to St. Petersburg this month. He was seventy-nine years of age and sixty-one years in Franciscan profession at the time of his death.[186]

A few weeks after the passing of Father Carol, the Mariological Society had its annual convention on May 30–31, 1990, in Providence. "The members remembered their founder at the celebration of the Eucharist and made plans for tributes to

---

[184] See Paul J. Spaeth, "History of the Franciscan Institute Library." (Bonaventure, NY, Bonaventure University, *Franciscan Studies* 51, 1991), 69–82.

[185] See Carol, *Fundamentals,* ix.

[186] Flavian A. Walsh, O.F.M. Provincial Vicar, (Holy Name Province, April 9,1990): Letter of Father Carol's passing, 1.

him at the 1991 and 1992
meetings."[187]

In 1991, *Marian Studies* published its forty-second issue
in which Father McCurry fondly remembers Carol in his article
entitled "Fr. Juniper B. Carol, O.F.M., 1911-1990: Vir
Catholicus Et Totus Apostolicus."[188] Father McCurry reflected
upon Father Carol with care and reverence, but he didn't shy
away from sharing a few very human qualities about him. One
story recounts the time Father McCurry offered to copy some
pages of Scotus' commentaries if Father Carol so wished.
"Long after he hopped his train for Florida, weeks and
thousands of photocopied pages later, I posted packet upon
packet to this 'apostolic' bibliographer without peer. His prompt
"thank you" note was signed "Scotistically Yours, Juniper."[189] I
found this story appealing because it gave me something person
about Carol that I had not read in any of his Marian
publications. McCurry discloses a couple more authentic
moments writing, "So what if he had a phobia of airplanes, a
propensity to misspell names, an intolerance of pettiness."[190]
McCurry didn't spend too much time making light of Carol.
Overall the article gives a beautiful homage to Father Juniper
Carol.

The passing of Father Juniper Carol in 1990 was
somewhat unexpected since he was simply recuperating from
prostate surgery. While he was sick for a time, his recovery was
seemingly within reach, but was simply not to be. Walsh writes,
"Juniper was waked on April 3 at Holy Name Friary in

---

[187] Koehler, "In Homage to the Founder of the Mariological Society of America,"
712.

[188] McCurry, "Fr. Juniper B. Carol, O.F.M., 1911–1990," *MS,* 1991. 9-14.

[189] McCurry, "Fr. Juniper B. Carol, O.F.M., 1911–1990," *MS,* 1991. 9.

[190] McCurry, "Fr. Juniper B. Carol, O.F.M., 1911–1990," 11.

Ringwood, and his funeral Mass was celebrated there on April 4 with Fr. Neil Padden as homilist. I have not been able to find a copy of this homily currently. At his own request, Juniper was cremated, and the ashes were buried in Holy Sepulcher Cemetery in Totowa, N.J. May Juniper rest in peace."[191]

Father Theodore A. Koehler. S.M. remembers the words written by John Joseph Cardinal Wright about Father Carol. Cardinal Wright said:

> By ancestry he is heir to the blood of Spain and therefore lightens his labor with that ardent love for the Queen of Heaven, which has warmed the songs of Spain and fired the speculations of her great theologians. By spiritual genealogy he is a son of the Franciscan family, a kinsman of those friars who, in every age and land, have preached love of Mary together with love for her Son. Out of the blend of these temperamental and spiritual influences there has come the predilection for reflection on and study of the mysteries surrounding Mary which has dominated his priestly work.[192]

Due to the progression of time, there are not a lot of people left who can speak lucidly about the man Father Juniper Carol. I have added in appendix A, B, and C some accounts of personal interviews I conducted with the few priests and religious I could find that knew him.

---

[191] Flavian A. Walsh, O.F.M. Provincial Vicar, (Holy Name Province, April 9,1990): Letter of Father Carol's passing, 2.

[192] Koehler, Theodore A., "In Homage to the Founder of the Mariological Society of America," *Marianum* LIII (1991): 713.

Father Carol's passion for publishing and furthering scholastic work on Mary to the English-speaking world is a valued contribution to Mariology. In the next chapter we will look a bit more into the first Marian topic that offers such a valued contribution, the Predestination of Mary.

THE PREDESTINATION OF MARY

Fr. Andrew Seebold, SM; Fr. Philip Hoelle, SM;
Fr. Juniper B. Carol, O.F.M; Fr. John Elbert, SM

1.17. Overview

Having discussed the life of Father Carol in Chapter 2, and after personally reading Father Juniper Carol's Marian publications, I have settled upon three primary areas of emphasis for his Mariology. According to me this is what he spent most of his time working on, but it is also the equivalent of a summary of Carol's Mariology. The first area of emphasis addresses the Predestination of Mary with her Son, with the second concerning the matter of Mary's preservative redemption, specifically addressing the matter of the *debitum peccati*, and finally Mary's participation in the salvific work of Jesus as Coredemptrix. While I have chosen to look at these themes, they are by no means his only contributions to the Marian field of scholarly work, nor do they minimize his great love for dogmatic theology as a whole. The reason for emphasizing these areas is in part due to Carol's areas of interest as demonstrated in his publications from 1936-1986. Before each doctrinal review I will list the publications featured in that chapter, and then examine the primary written contributions he made to that field, remembering McCurry who wrote in the 1991 edition of *Marian Studies*, "Fr. Juniper's main contributions on these themes would not seem to be in the originality of his analysis but in the integrity of his synthesis."[193]

---

[193] McCurry, "Fr. Juniper B. Carol, O.F.M., 1911–1990," 12–13. Remember, according to McCurry, these themes refer to Mary's Mediation connected to the foot of the cross, and her Immaculate Conception understood in relation to Christ's primacy.

Carol will spend most of his life publishing on the Predestination of Mary with her Son, the *debitum peccati* and Coredemption, even after Vatican II. Carol's overall Mariology summarized in the three themes seems to be consistent from the early years to his later years, and his doctrinal emphasis in publishing does not change; rather, he expands the content (for example, dealing with the predestination of Mary, Carol in, *The Absolute Primacy and Predestination of Jesus and His Virgin Mother*, 1981, looks at the Franciscan and Thomistic perspectives of the Predestination of Jesus and Mary. Carol gives an overview of the topic from the fifteenth to the twentieth century. In 1986, Carol in *Why Jesus Christ? Thomistic, Scotistic and Conciliatory Perspectives*, refers to the previous works, then expands the topic with more references.), of his earlier publications.

When the young Carol was asked what discipline he would choose to focus upon as a teacher, Carol states, "I would choose Dogmatic Theology because I feel a strong liking for it and believe I will be more successful studying it than any other subject."[194] Carol's publications in the area of Dogmatic Theology, specifically Mariology is a valued contribution to this field and one that he did consistently throughout his life. His interest in Mariology as demonstrated in his careful solicitation of academics for the *Marian Studies* publications, and his numerous publications on Mary and bibliographical works have provided a wealth of resources for students and theologians alike. Carol was not simply tied down to these three Marian themes of the Predestination of Mary with her Son, the *debitum* and Coredemption, yet I find that the areas I will emphasize

---

[194] Juniper B. Carol, O.F.M., "Questionnaire For IV Year Theologians," (1935), 1.

within Carol's Mariology others have seen as well. Father McCurry said about Carol's Mariology:

> The main themes that he derived from his rigorous study of the Catholic mariological tradition were: first, the Blessed Virgin's Mediation—which always includes her unique role at the foot of the Cross; and the second her Immaculate Conception—which must be always understood in relationship to the Primacy of Christ. Fr. Juniper's main contributions on these themes would not seem to be in the originality of his analysis but in the integrity of his synthesis.[195]

McCurry mentions Mary's Mediation, which according to his understanding of Carol would always include her at the foot of the cross, and the Immaculate Conception, which encompasses her separation from the effects of Original Sin. The three Marian areas Carol published on, which I focus on in this thesis include those which McCurry highlights. McCurry quotes Carol, who would state that all Marian explanations could be reduced to, "The absolute and universal primacy of Christ.[196] Again, McCurry states that Carol's "Substance-his intellectual priorities and apostolate- was securely focused on one goal above all: the Primacy of Jesus Christ."[197] I believe the three Marian topics I explore all fall under this category of the Primacy of Jesus Christ.

Starting with the predestation of Mary, then examining Adamic sin and our redemption, along with Mary's preservative

---

195 McCurry, "Fr. Juniper B. Carol, O.F.M., 1911–1990," 12–13.
196 McCurry, "Fr. Juniper B. Carol, O.F.M., 1911–1990," 11."
197 McCurry, "Fr. Juniper B. Carol, O.F.M., 1911–1990," 11.

redemption, this thesis will then look Carol's efforts in promoting Our Lady as Coredemptrix. Each of these topics is extremely dense in theological insights and developments, and consequently, can have a significant impact for our spirituality. Difficulties in explaining them in a polished way is not mine alone. As St. Anselm says:

> I am afraid that, just as I am invariably annoyed by bad painters when I see the Lord himself depicted as of ugly appearance, the same fault will be found with me, if I presume to plough through such beautiful subject-matter with an unpolished and contemptible style of writing.[198]

With Father Carol as a reference I shall examine the predestination of Mary, the *debitum* and Coredemption in greater depth.

In this third chapter, the primary texts referenced in this annotated bibliography for Mary's predestination, spanning from 1956-1986, will be:[199]

1956

Fundamentals of Mariology, New York, Benziger, 1956, pp. i–203. This is a book providing the primary fundamentals of Mariology Carol taught which would teach seminarians, religious and priests. It is referenced here because of his

---

[198] Brian Davis, and G.R. Evans, ed., *Anselm of Canterbury The Major Works*, (NY, Oxford University Press, 1998), 267.

[199] At the end of the chapter a continued list of Carol's works dealing with the topic will be given. This is only for the reader to explore further works published by Carol and will not be analyzed.

treatment of Mary's predestation, looking at four propositions for this. Both the Franciscan and Thomistic views given.

1980

"The Absolute Predestination of the Blessed Virgin Mary", *Marian Studies* 31 (1980): 172–238. This article looks at modern authors in 19th and 20th centuries. Primarily favoring the Scotistic thought that predominately supports perspectives of Mary's predestination. He does give a couple Thomistic perspectives. There are hundreds of references for further reading on this subject at the end of the article.

1981

The Absolute Primacy and Predestination of Jesus and His Virgin Mother, (Chicago: Franciscan Herald Press, 1981), i, 1–177. This book looks at the Franciscan and Thomistic perspectives of the predestination of Jesus and Mary. From an overview of the Franciscan and Thomistic debate, Carol looks at Scotus and then gives an overview of the topic from the fifteenth to the twentieth century.

1986

Why Jesus Christ? Thomistic, Scotistic and Conciliatory Perspectives, (Manassas, Virginia: Trinity Communications, 1986), xvii, 1–531.[200] This is the culmination of the previous works, inclusive of their primary content and expanded with more references. The Thomistic school is represented and the

---

[200] Fr. Gambero puts this under 1985, but Fehlner under 1986. The actual publication date is 1986.

Scotistic follows in the publication. Carol's conclusions on this topic do not vary from earlier publications.

1.18. The Predestined Primacy of Mary with Jesus

According to Carol, Mary is the recipient of the Trinity's generosity in the most unique way.[201] She now stands as an icon for the Church; a standard, but always our Mother, leading us into greater intimate response (*anabasis*) and elevation, due to the descent (*katabasis*) or condescension of God in Christ.[202] In her, we are nurtured to a greater reception of Christ in the sacraments of the Church, and become more receptive to the Spirit's unfolding of the life of Christ within us.

Our Lady is not predestined due to any merit upon her own; rather, it is entirely gratuitous upon the part of God. According to Carol, it is God who intentionally wills Mary's predestination. In his book, *Fundamentals of Mariology* he states the following:

> If, in point of time, we find Our Blessed Lady
> fulfilling a specific mission entrusted to her by
> the Almighty, it is obvious that this mission is
> the result of a positive act on the part of God's
> will from all eternity. This divine will,
> determining the existence of Our Lady, ordaining
> her to the beatific vision and (as a means to the
> end) charging her with a specific function in the

---

[201] See Father Juniper Carol, O.F.M., "Our Lady's Immunity From The Debt Of Sin," *Marian Studies* 6 (1955): 165.

[202] See Philippians 2.6-8

divine economy is what we mean here by her predestination.[203]

The book, *Fundamentals of Mariology*, was published in 1956 and is essentially a primer on Marian teachings. This work is helpful because here we can see what he would teach and lecture students concerning specific Mariological topics.[204] Usually the classes were attended by graduate students, sisters, and a few priests and seminarians.[205] While the book *Fundamentals* is less in depth concerning the predestination of Mary with Jesus than the work, "The Absolute Predestination of the Blessed Virgin Mary" he contributed to *Marian Studies* in 1980, and smaller than the massive opus *Why Jesus Christ?*, published in 1986 it is still important because we can see that his emphasis on this topic did not change or decrease, even after Vatican II., rather his attention and emphasis in publication expands this topic further than *Fundamentals*. What Carol teaches priests and seminarians about Mary's predestination in his fundamental Mariology course and the book *Fundamentals* is what we see in greater depth in his later works.

According to Carol in *Fundamentals of Mariology*, he gives four propositions for Mary's predestination, with the first

---

[203] Carol, *Fundamentals,* 21. This chapter distinguishes four propositions within her predestination. 1. The order of intention. 2. Jesus and Mary predestined in one and the same decree. 3. With and under Christ she has priority in predestination. 4. Her predestination is secondary cause of all others' predestination. First two accepted by most scholars. The latter two are primarily held by Franciscans., 21–25.

[204] Carol, *Fundamentals*, ix. "The present book aims to satisfy the repeated requests addressed to the author from various quarters, urging him to publish the series of Mariology lectures which he offers regularly at St. Bonaventure University."

[205] See, Carol, *Fundamentals*, ix.

two, according to Carol accepted by all and the latter two principally held by Franciscans.[206]

The first proposition for the predestation of Mary according to Carol in *Fundamentals of Mariology*, states that the predestination of Mary was an "absolutely gratuitous act on the part of God. That means that Our Lady did not merit this Maternity *in the order of intention*, as the Schoolmen say."[207] This divine maternity is that from which all her merit springs and therefore cannot be something she gained on her own. Father Carol says,

> However, theologians generally admit that Mary merited the divine Maternity in the order of execution; not in strict justice, but only out of fittingness. In other words, once God had decreed to make Mary the Mother of His Son, He gave her the grace to merit that high degree of sanctity and purity, which would render her worthy to be the Mother of God.[208]

Carol's second proposition for the predestination of Mary states, "The Blessed Virgin was predestined to the divine Maternity in one and the same decree with Christ. This is the teaching of Pius IX in the bull *Ineffabilis Deus* (December 8, 1854), and of Pius XII in the bull *Munificentissimus Deus* (November 1, 1950). Both states unequivocally that Jesus and Mary were predestined 'uno eodemque decreto.' (one and the

---

[206] See Carol, *Fundamentals*, 21.
[207] Carol, *Fundamentals*, 21.
[208] Carol, *Fundamentals*, 22.

same decree).[209] This may be gathered also from Sacred Scripture."[210]

The third proposition for the predestination of Mary states, "With and under Christ, the Blessed Virgin was predestined with a logical priority to all others."[211] Carol then references St. Thomas in, *Contra Gentiles* and encourages readers to read W. Allen's article, "The Predestination of Mary in the Light of Modern Controversy", published in the 1951 *Marian Studies* for the reader to gain understanding in the Thomistic view of predestination.[212] Carol wraps up his third proposition for the predestination of Mary by saying, "Since Mother and Son were predestined in one and the same decree, it follows that the above reasoning applies also-with proper subordination—to Our Blessed Lady. Consequently, her predestination (the same as Christ's) could not have been conditioned upon that of Adam and Eve or any other creature. It was the other way around."[213]

The fourth proposition for the predestination of Mary, according to Carol says:

> The predestination of the Blessed Virgin was the secondary cause of the predestination of all others. This thesis is a necessary corollary of the above. Christ is the primary exemplary cause of our predestination, as we gather from St. Paul: "For those whom he has foreknown, he has also

---

209 Latin translation in parenthesis done through Yandex Translate: https://translate.yandex.com/?lang=la-en&text=uno%20eodemque%20decreto

210 Carol, *Fundamentals*., 22.

211 Carol, *Fundamentals*, 22.

212 Allen, W. *The Predestination of Mary in the Light of Modern Controversy,* in *MS*, 2 (1951), 178–92.

213 Carol, *Fundamentals*, 23.

predestined to become conformed to the image of his Son" (Romans 8:29). Christ is likewise the efficient cause of our predestination because He merited it for us. Lastly, He is the final cause of our predestination inasmuch as we are all predestined for His honor and glory. Now, since the Blessed Virgin shares the primacy of Christ in the eternal decrees of God, she must share also the causality of her Son with regard to all others. In other words, we are all indebted to her, after Christ, for our own predestination.[214]

The four propositions of Mary's predestination reference some authors that Carol will give more attention to in the 1980 publication, "The Absolute Predestination of the Blessed Virgin Mary," found in *Marian Studies*. There are many theologians Carol will continue to reference in his decades-long development of the doctrine of Mary's predestination with her Son, such as the French theologian, Fr. J. F. Bonnefoy, O.F.M. (A Franciscan, who published on this topic of Mary's predestination in *Mariology*, vol. 2, "Predestination of Our Lady."), and the theologians Rocca (A Servite priest, and professor at the International College of Servites in Rome, and published many Marian works) and Roschini (1900-1977-A Servite priest, Italian, Founder of the Marianum, and professor of Mariology. He published over 900 titles, and worked with the Vatican on Marian publications), the latter (Roschini) who according to Carol, "partially endorsed" Bonnefoy's theory.[215] He also mentions, as previously stated, W. Allen's work in *Marian Studies* published in 1951, "The Predestination of Mary

---

[214] Carol, *Fundamentals*, 24–25.
[215] Carol, *Fundamentals*, footnote 32. 24.

in the Light of Modern Controversy," so the reader can find the "opposite" view (Thomistic school), according to Carol.[216]

In *Marian Studies* 31, published in 1980, almost 25 years after *Fundamentals*, Carol writes more in depth about Mary's predestination. Father Carol says the following concerning Our Lady's predestination:

> It is precisely the stand we take on this subject that will set virtually every other mariological thesis in its proper perspective. The unique place held by Mary in the overall hierarchy of beings making up the entire creation is bound to give cohesion and unity to the scientific structure of the Marian tract.[217]

In the beginning of this article Carol references his 1956 book, *Fundamentals* in reference to the questions theologians discuss when speaking of Mary's predestination, but he doesn't in this article go into any of the details of the four points which he developed in the book, except one. Carol does say, "the only one that concerns us here is the exact place assigned to her in the internal hierarchy of the divine decree relative to the universe. Briefly: whether or not Mary was willed (predestined) by God with a *logical priority* over all other creatures."[218] When Carol uses the word predestination, he has a specific definition in mind. "By "predestination" we mean the eternal act of God's will determining the existence of a rational creature and

---

[216] Carol, *Fundamentals*, 23 (footnote 32).

[217] Father Juniper Carol, O.F.M., "The Absolute Predestination of The Blessed Virgin Mary", *Marian Studies* 31 (1980): 178.

[218] Carol, "The Absolute Predestination of The Blessed Virgin Mary", 178.

ordaining it to grace and glory."[219] In this work, Carol believes that in order to look at Mary's predestination we must address Christ's own predestination, and specifically the reason for the Incarnation. Carol writes, "Since Mary's predestination is but one aspect of the broader question of Christ's own predestination, the former must perforce be treated within that frame of reference."[220] In light of this, Carol will look at the Thomistic and Franciscan theories on the primary reason for the Incarnation.[221]

Carol gives seven theories on the primary reason for the Incarnation, each with its own conclusion. Really, this article gives a brief overview of a couple Thomistic theories on the reason for the Incarnation and then almost fifty pages highlighting those theologians who support the Franciscan view.[222] Carol writes, "We propose to offer: (a) a synopsis of the various opinions on the primary reason for the Incarnation and (b) a list of modern authors (nineteenth and twentieth centuries) who, in our judgment, have endorsed, at least in substance, what is commonly known as the "Franciscan" viewpoint relative to the role of Christ and His Mother in the internal hierarchy of the divine decree concerning the universe."[223]

The first theory on the Incarnation presented in the article, "The Absolute Predestination of The Blessed Virgin

---

[219] Father Juniper Carol, O.F.M., "The Absolute Predestination of The Blessed Virgin Mary", *Marian Studies* 31 (1980): 178. (From now on, Carol, "The Absolute Predestination of The Blessed Virgin Mary").

[220] Carol, "The Absolute Predestination of The Blessed Virgin Mary", 178.

[221] See Carol, "The Absolute Predestination of The Blessed Virgin Mary", 178.

[222] See Carol, "The Absolute Predestination of The Blessed Virgin Mary", 235.

[223] Carol, "The Absolute Predestination of The Blessed Virgin Mary", 180.

Mary" is a Thomistic perspective, according to Carol, and it states the following:

1. "God decrees to create the universe in order to manifest His goodness.
2. God decrees the permission of Adam's sin.
3. God decrees to become man (Incarnation) in order to redeem man."[224]

Carol's first theory posits the viewpoint of followers of St. Thomas Aquinas concerning the primary reason for the Incarnation but does not give specifics as to who is included in this first group. He writes, "The only primary reason for the Incarnation is man's Redemption. Hence, if Adam had not sinned, there would have been no Incarnation."[225] In this first section, Carol does address an idea by the Dominican, G. Friethoff, who, according to Carol, thought Friethoff, "suspects that it may be even heretical (!) to assign the Incarnation any reason other than man's redemption,"[226] To which Carol reminds the reader:

> For St. Thomas, the ultimate reason for the
> Incarnation is God's infinite goodness (CF.
> Summa, III, q. 1, a. 1). We have it on the
> authority of Benedict XIV that Dominicans and
> Franciscans were forbidden by Pope Sixtus IV to
> call one another 'heretics' in this connection,
> since, as he put it, the opinions held by both

---

[224] Carol, "The Absolute Predestination of The Blessed Virgin Mary", 180–81.

[225] Carol, "The Absolute Predestination of The Blessed Virgin Mary", 181.

[226] Carol, "The Absolute Predestination of The Blessed Virgin Mary", 181. Footnote 7,

groups 'are based on piety, the authorities of faith, and reasons.'[227]

There is only one perspective regarding the first theory given by Carol to defend that Thomistic view concerning the Incarnation.

According to Carol, the second Thomistic theory has the following points for the Incarnation. He posits the following:

1. "In the order of final causality, Christ is willed first.
2. In the order of material causality, the Redemption is willed first."[228]

According to Aristotle, a corruptible substance must depend on some other substance that produced it. This gives us the idea of final causality.[229] Material causality has its origin in Aristotle's efficient causal definition which states an action can be a cause.[230] The conclusion from this second Thomistic theory according to Carol is that the Incarnation is the final cause of creation as a whole, but redemption is the material cause of the Incarnation. Both of the first two theories as articulated by Carol claim their opinions are based on Aquinas.[231] Here Carol says this theory is endorsed by Thomists such as, Cardinal Cajetan (Italian Cardinal, Master General of the Dominican order, (1469-1534), primarily known for opposition to Martin Luther's teachings), the Salmanticenses (The college at Salamanca and those within held and promoted Scholastic theology. Strict

---

[227] Carol, "The Absolute Predestination of The Blessed Virgin Mary", 181. Footnote 7.

[228] Carol, "The Absolute Predestination of The Blessed Virgin Mary"181.

[229] See, Encyclopedia.com, https://www.encyclopedia.com/religion/encyclopedias-almanacs-transcripts-and-maps/final-causality

[230] See, Wikipedia, https://en.wikipedia.org/wiki/Causality

[231] See Carol, "The Absolute Predestination of The Blessed Virgin Mary", 181 82

adherents to Thomism.),[232] Capreolus (John Capreolus was a French theologian and Dominican, 1380-1444. Known as the "Prince of Thomists."),[233] Medina (Juan de Medina, 1490-1547, theologian and professor, from Spain.),[234] Gonet (Jean Baptiste Gonet, 1616-1681, Dominican, Priest, Provincial, and professor.),[235] and others.[236]

In the third theory for the Incarnation, Carol looks at Scotus and his followers order of predestinations.[237]

1. "God decrees the existence of Christ, independently of any other circumstance, in order to have someone who will love Him in a most perfect way.
2. God decrees the existence of angels and men, with Christ as their final, exemplary and efficient (meritorious) cause.
3. God decrees the rest of the universe for the glory of Christ.
4. God decrees the permission of Adam's sin.
5. God decrees that Christ will come *in carne passibili* (in the flesh) as Redeemer."[238]

This third theory concludes, according to the conclusion of Carol in *The Absolute Predestination of The Blessed Virgin Mary*, that "Even if Adam had not sinned, God would have become incarnate, not as Redeemer, of course, but as King of all creation."[239] The primary people holding this theory was followers of Bl. John Duns Scotus, O.F.M. (1265-1308), born in

---

[232] See, New Advent, http://www.newadvent.org/cathen/13401c.htm
[233] See, New Advent, http://www.newadvent.org/cathen/03314a.htm
[234] See, New Advent, http://www.newadvent.org/cathen/10144a.htm
[235] See, New Advent, http://www.newadvent.org/cathen/06634a.htm
[236] Carol, "The Absolute Predestination of The Blessed Virgin Mary", 181.
[237] See Carol, "The Absolute Predestination of The Blessed Virgin Mary", 182.
[238] Carol, "The Absolute Predestination of The Blessed Virgin Mary", 182.
[239] Carol, "The Absolute Predestination of The Blessed Virgin Mary", 182.

Scotland, enters Order of Friars Minor at 15, championed the Immaculate Conception),[240] and a few who were not Franciscan, such as A. Catharinus, O.P., A. Salmeron, S.J. (Alfonso Salmeron, born in Spain, 1515-1585. Biblical scholar, priest and one of the first Jesuits),[241] St. Francis de Sales (Jesuit priest, 1567-1622, author of *Introduction to the Devout Life*, originally from France and eventually became bishop of Geneva.)[242], etc.[243]

The fourth theory promulgated by Francisco Suarez, S.J. (d. 1617) (Suarez, a Jesuit, philosopher, theologian, priest and professor. Highly respected, started a school of his own thought, "Suarism", and some (Mackintosh) consider him a founder of International law.)[244], looks at an attempt to harmonize the Thomists and Scotists in what is called the "Conciliatory Opinion."[245] The primary points are the following:

1. "The intrinsic excellence of the mystery itself, and
2. The Redemption of the world."[246]

Thus, according to this fourth principle the Incarnation would have taken place independent of Adam's sin since either reason would work. Father Carol writes, "This opinion never found a sufficient number of adherents to form a School—not even within the Society of Jesus."[247]

---

[240] See, EWTN.com, http://www.ewtn.com/library/mary/scotus.htm
[241] See, Wikipedia, https://en.wikipedia.org/wiki/Alfonso_Salmeron
[242] See, Franciscanmedia.org, https://www.franciscanmedia.org/saint-francis-de-sales/
[243] See Carol, "The Absolute Predestination of The Blessed Virgin Mary", 182-183.
[244] See, New Advent, http://www.newadvent.org/cathen/14319a.htm
[245] See Carol, "The Absolute Predestination of The Blessed Virgin Mary", 183.
[246] Carol, "The Absolute Predestination of The Blessed Virgin Mary", 183.
[247] Carol, "The Absolute Predestination of The Blessed Virgin Mary", 184.

The fifth perspective addressing the order of predestinations is from J.F. Bonnefoy, O.F.M.:[248]

1. "God decrees the Incarnation as the highest possible communication of His goodness in order to have someone who will love Him in a supreme way.

2. God decrees the existence of Mary, Christ's associate, so that Christ may have a most perfect beneficiary with whom He may share His goodness and happiness.

3. God decrees the existence of angels and men, so that Christ and Mary may have beneficiaries on whom they may bestow their gifts.

4. God decrees the existence of the material universe, destined to be the throne and footstool of His Son (Acts 9:49).

5. Since it is nobler to dispense one's own gifts than those belonging to others, God decrees that Christ and Mary will earn (merit) such gifts for their beneficiaries.

6. Since the most excellent way to show one's love is to lay down one's life for the loved ones (John 15:13), God decrees Christ's sufferings and death, with Mary's share therein.

7. Since it is more noble and perfect 'to forgive' than 'to give,' God decrees (with a permissive will) the fall of our first parents so as to make possible the Redemption (and Coredemption) from sin, as the 'perfect gift' to Christ's and Mary's beneficiaries."[249]

---

[248] Carol makes it clear that Bonnefoy really develops and systematizes this theory more than authors it. (see footnote 16 in "The Absolute Predestination). Concerning Bonnefoy, his article, "The Presentation of Our Blessed Lady" was published in *Mariology*, vol. 2 in 1957.

[249] Carol, "The Absolute Predestination of The Blessed Virgin Mary", 185.

In response to the question of whether the Incarnation would have taken place independent of Adam's sin, Carol argues Bonnefoy's point. Carol writes, "To the hypothetical question, 'Would the Incarnation have taken place if Adam had not sinned?' Bonnefoy answers: The problem should not be formulated hypothetically, since God has not revealed what He might have done (or not done) in an order of things different from the one He actually chose."[250] According to Carol these views have been supported by modern authors such as Alonso, Bertetto, Leblond, O'Neill, and E. Schmidt.[251]

The sixth theory is that of the theologians Rocca–Roschini, which states, "The primary reason for the Incarnation is: God's free election of the present order, in which the Incarnation is decreed *independently* of Adam's sin but *connected* with it."[252] In response to the hypothetical question on whether God would have become incarnate had Adam not sinned, Carol quotes the authors Rocca and Roschini state: "We do not know for certain, since God has not revealed to us what He might have done (or not done) in an order different from the one He actually chose."[253]

The final theory for the Incarnation in Carol's article, "The Absolute Predestination of the Blessed Virgin Mary," is based on W. H. Marshner's position. According to Carol, Marshner's position states:

1. "In a logically early moment God knows, through His *scientia simplicis intelligentiae*, (the knowledge of simple

---

[250] Carol, "The Absolute Predestination of The Blessed Virgin Mary", 186.

[251] See Carol, "The Absolute Predestination of The Blessed Virgin Mary", 186.

[252] Carol, "The Absolute Predestination of The Blessed Virgin Mary", 187.

[253] Carol, "The Absolute Predestination of The Blessed Virgin Mary", 187.

intelligence) all possible worlds, with different ones presumably having different things to recommend them.

2. Among these possible worlds which God understands, there is one in which a race is raised to friendship with Him through capitulation in its first parent. Still through His *scientia simplicis intelligentiae*, He understands the possible loss of that friendship, and its possible restoration through the Logos, become incarnate.

3. God prefers this possible world because of the infinite glory resulting from the redemptive Incarnation which is a feature of it.

4. God chooses to create this particular world, and through His *scientia visionis*, (science of vision) He knows all that His creation will contain relative to each efficacious decree."[254]

5. Father Carol compares this with the Scotus schema stating, "that the divine volition, in proceeding *ad extra*, begins not with an Incarnation willed in isolation, but willed within a set of possible worlds of which the Incarnation is a feature, although the set is chosen *because* of that feature (i.e., the Incarnation)."[255]

Carol concludes with the following twelve-point analysis of such a schema:

1. "The reason God chose to create a world such as ours is that the Incarnation might occur.

2. Since the Incarnation is the final cause of creation, it should form the content of the very first of God's efficacious decrees *in ordine intentionis*. (In the order of intention).

---

[254] Carol, "The Absolute Predestination of The Blessed Virgin Mary", 187.
[255] Carol, "The Absolute Predestination of The Blessed Virgin Mary", 188.

3. The Incarnation thus chosen first, and for the sake of which all else will follow, is already a redemptive Incarnation.

4. Adam, his fall, and his descendants are already *praeintellecta* (as opposed to *praevisa*) as features of a merely possible world which might be made to exist for the sake of a redemptive Incarnation.

5. There is no particular difficulty about picking a possible descendant of Adam (who will exist if she is chosen to cooperate in the Incarnation) as a second criterion for choosing to create the possible world in which she will exist.

6. Mary's existence as Theotokos-Coredemptrix would thereby form a secondary and further-determining reason for the creation of just *this* world.

7. The predestination of Mary's existence and privileges could thereby form the secondary content of the very first of God's efficacious decrees *in ordine intentionis*. (the order of intent).

8. Mary, who had already been *praeintellecta* as a descendant of fallen Adam, is now *praevisa* as such a descendant. But this does not mean that she is now included in Adam's moral headship and thus subject to the universal law of sin, because there are no subjections to laws outside efficacious decrees, and neither Adam nor his fall has yet been efficaciously decreed.

9. When Adam is efficaciously decreed in solidarity with 'many,' he and they are decreed for the sake of Christ and Mary. Her logically antecedent predestination prevents Mary from being among the 'many.'

10. Nevertheless, *de potentia ordinata*, God could have actualized a theologically possible world one of whose

features could have been God's pre-vision of Mary as contracting original sin.

11. Therefore, while utterly exempt from all *debitum peccati* (because efficaciously decreed with a logical priority to the absolute prevision of the Fall) her predestination is nevertheless a redemption because she was *praeintellecta* (and could have been *praevisa*) as forming part of a theologically possible world in which she could have contracted original sin.

12. Finally, the Mary who was de facto predestined as Mother of the Savior, and about whom the *debitum* controversy is waged, is not the 'Mary' who could have contracted original sin in a theologically possible world. The latter 'Mary' was the object of God's *scientia simplicis intelligentiae*, never the object of His *scientia visionis*."[256]

Father Carol concludes by reminding the reader that all of these theories state that Mary "was predestined 'in one and the same decree' with Christ. As a consequence, for the Thomists, if Adam had not sinned, Mary would not have existed—a conclusion logically rejected by the exponents of Theory (c)[257] above."[258]

The work of Father Carol in this Marian teaching alone is quite extensive. He refers the reader to numerous pages of modern Franciscan supporters of the Franciscan viewpoint referenced above. He states:

> Our survey, which covers only the nineteenth and twentieth centuries, includes 504 authors. Of these, many are well-known and respected

---

[256] Carol, "The Absolute Predestination of The Blessed Virgin Mary", 188–89.

[257] It is marked as point 3 for me.

[258] Carol, "The Absolute Predestination of The Blessed Virgin Mary", 189.

professional theologians, others would fall under the category of spiritual writers."[259]

Carol then writes:

> Of the 504 authors mentioned, 214 belong to the Franciscan Order. That should surprise no one, since the doctrine of Christ's and Mary's absolute and universal primacy has always been cherished by the spiritual sons of the Poverello. The remaining 290 belong to various Religious Orders (Jesuits, Benedictines, Mercedarians, etc.) and to the diocesan clergy, with a few lay writers added. This should dispose of the claim sometimes made that the Franciscan viewpoint is endorsed only by the members of the Seraphic Order 'and a few others.'[260]

While there are many variations found within this doctrinal presentation, even between Bonnefoy, Rocca–Roschini, and Marshner, they all share according to Carol a uniformity of beliefs on three important points:[261]

1. "Christ and Mary hold an ontological primacy (not only a primacy of honor) over all creation;
2. They were predestined with a logical priority over the rest of the predestined; and
3. As a result of the above, they were predestined independently of Adam's sin."[262]

---

[259] Carol, "The Absolute Predestination of The Blessed Virgin Mary", 235.

[260] Carol, "The Absolute Predestination of The Blessed Virgin Mary", 235.

[261] See Carol, "The Absolute Predestination of The Blessed Virgin Mary", 238.

[262] See Carol, "The Absolute Predestination of The Blessed Virgin Mary", 238.

Father Carol prefers Professor Marshner's theory,[263] but he is careful to extend honor and proper representation to the varying perspectives.

While looking at numerous Magisterial passages and a few theologians who speak about the importance of the primacy and predestination of Jesus with his mother, it should be noted that Father Carol continued to publish on the topic of Mary's predestination until the mid-1980s. In 1981, Carol wrote, *The Absolute Primacy and Predestination of Jesus and His Virgin Mother*. This was published by Franciscan Herald Press and treats the topic of the predestination of Jesus and Mary in a more complete way than the earlier article published with *Marian Studies* in 1980. Yet, Carol does give the exact same reasons for the Incarnation by the Thomists that he did in "The Absolute Predestination of The Blessed Virgin Mary."[264] For the Franciscan perspective Carol again refers to Bonnefoy,[265] Rocca and Roschini[266] and W.H. Marshner.[267] After this, Carol examines the predecessors of Scotus in the second part of the book. From the seventh century with Isaac of Niniveh[268] Carol continues up to the 19th century followed by almost fifty pages of supporters of the Franciscan perspective, where he says, "It would be beyond the scope of our study to expand on the subject. In all justice, however, explicit mention must be made here of the several scholars who contributed most to the

---

[263] See Carol, "The Absolute Predestination of The Blessed Virgin Mary", 238. A small aside. William H. Marshner writes the Prefatory Note in Carol's book, The Absolute Primacy and Predestination of Jesus and His Virgin Mother. Iv-vi.

[264] See *The Absolute Primacy and Predestination of Jesus and His Virgin Mother*, Chicago, Franciscan Herald Press, 1981, pp 9-10.

[265] See *The Absolute Primacy and Predestination of Jesus and His Virgin Mother*, Chicago, Franciscan Herald Press, 1981, pp.13-14. (Henceforth cited as, Carol, Primacy).

[266] Carol, *Primacy* 15.

[267] Carol, *Primacy* 15.

[268] Carol, *Primacy* 19.

dissemination of our Franciscan thesis between 1900 and the present date (1981)."[269]. In Juniper Carol's book, *Why Jesus Christ?* Carol expends even more on the topic of the predestination of Mary and Jesus, focusing more on why the Incarnation occurs from a Thomistic and Franciscan perspective. This treatment gave more time to the Thomistic view, over 100 pages, but even in this book, the Thomistic perspective is only a third of what is given to the Franciscan position. Carol's presentation of Mary's predestination does not change; rather, he continues to enhance and focus even more on reasons why the Franciscan view is so favorably held by so many theologians, both from the past and up to the time of the publication of his book, *Why Jesus Christ?* in 1986.

Here are a few of Carol's publications for further review of the Primacy and predestination of Jesus and His Mother that show Carol's continued interest in the topic. This annotated bibliography of books, (the book reviews are not annotated) gives a small brief for the readers' sake:

1956

Fundamentals of Mariology, New York, Benziger, 1956, pp. i, 1–203. This is a book providing the primary fundamentals of Mariology Carol taught which would teach seminarians, religious and priests. It is referenced here because of his treatment of Mary's predestination, looking at four propositions for this. Both the Franciscan and Thomistic view is given.

1980

"The Absolute Predestination of the Blessed Virgin Mary", *Marian Studies* 31 (1980): 172–238. This article looks at

---

[269] Carol, *Primacy* 96.

modern authors in 19th and 20th centuries. Primarily favoring the Scotistic thought that predominately support perspectives of Mary's predestination. He does give a couple Thomistic perspectives. There are hundreds of references for further reading on this subject at the end of the article.

1981

Michael Meilach: "Mary Immaculate in the Divine Plan," Wilmington, Delaware, 1981, pp. vi, 1–96. (Preface by J. B. Carol).

The Absolute Primacy and Predestination of Jesus and His Virgin Mother, Chicago, Franciscan Herald Press, 1981, pp. i, 1–177. This book looks at the Franciscan and Thomistic perspectives of the predestination of Jesus and Mary. From an overview of the Franciscan and Thomistic debate, Carol looks at Scotis and then gives an overview of the topic from the fifteenth to the twentieth century.

1982

"Cur Deus Homo?", *The Homiletic and Pastoral Review* 82 (August-September 1982), pp. 8–9.

1983

"Duns Scotus on the Incarnation," *The Homiletic and Pastoral Review* 83 (June 1983), P. 4.

1984

Francesco Saverio Pancheri, *The Universal Primacy of Christ*, translated and adapted from the Italian edition by J. B. Carol, O.F.M. (Front Royal, Virginia, Christendom 1984), x, 1-144.

Pancheri, O.F.M. Conv., is an Italian theologian who wrote his doctoral dissertation on Matthias Joseph Scheeben, and to Carol has written a clear analysis of the incongruities in the Scotistic theory of Christ's universal Primacy. Carol writes in the preface his reason another book on the subject is justified, "It offers, for the first time in the English language, a frank and objective analysis of the theological incongruities inherent in the traditional Scotistic theory to explain Christ's universal Primacy." 9.

1985

Predestination of Mary, iDictionary of Mary: "Behold Your Mother", (New York, Catholic Book Publishing Co., 1985), 273–275.

1986

Why Jesus Christ? Thomistic, Scotistic and Conciliatory Perspectives, (Manassas, Virginia, Trinity Communications, 1986), xvii, 1–531.[270] This is the culmination of the previous works, inclusive of their primary content and expanded with more references. The Thomistic school from is represented and the Scotistic follows. The later opinions of Carol on this topic do not vary from earlier publications.

---

[270] Fr. Gambero puts this under 1985, but Fehlner under 1986. The actual publication date is 1986.

DEBITUM PECCATI

Fr. Juniper B. Carol, O.F.M.

Having looked at the predestination of Mary and Jesus according to Carol, we will now look a bit deeper into the effects of sin and Mary's immunity from it. In that Mary has always been predestined with Jesus according Carol's presentation of the Franciscan perspectives previously discussed, it is from this that the discussion of the *Debitum Peccati* (debt of sin) becomes so important. Since she is predestined, Mary is free from the debt of sin, and this will be further explored in this fourth chapter. The primary texts we will look at which deal with Mary's immunity from actual sin are:

1955

"Our Lady's Immunity from the Debt of Sin," *Marian Studies* 6 (1955): 164–168. This article looks at Mary's Immunity from the debt of sin by looking at Mary's unique place in the hierarchy of creation. She belongs to the Hypostatic Order[271] according to Carol and is not subject to the debt of sin because of her predestination with Christ.

1956

Fundamentals of Mariology (New York: Benziger, 1956), xx, 1–203. This is a book providing the primary fundamentals of Mariology Carol taught which would teach seminarians, religious and priests. It is referenced here because of his

---

[271] "But she belongs to the Hypostatic Order inasmuch as it was in her and through her that the Union was accomplished." Carol, Immunity, 165.

treatment of the *Debitum Peccati* in the chapter, "Mary's Immunity from Actual Sin," 135-141.

1977

"The Blessed Virgin and the "Debitum Peccati." A Bibliographical Conspectus," *Marian Studies* 28 (1977), 181–256. This publication defines the *debitum* and addresses four responses to the understanding of the universal necessity to contract original sin concerning Mary. Then Carol provides a chronological bibliography of 564 theologians differentiating their opinions of the *debitum* by using eleven specific criteria.

1978

A History of the Controversy over the "Debitum Peccati", Franciscan Institute Publications. Theology Series, No. 9 (St. Bonaventure, NY.: The Franciscan Institute, 1978), xiii, 1–260. This book examines the topic of the *debitum* from the beginning (Augustine quoted for Carol's start point) and looks at primary religious figures who wrote on the topic. From Franciscans to Jesuits, key periods of debate and times of decline Carol explores the history of this controversy.

1979

"Reflections on the Problem of Mary's Preservative Redemption," *Marian Studies* 30 (1979): 19–88. This work looks at the teaching that denies Mary's redemption before the definition of the Immaculate Conception and after, and then the teaching that says Mary was redeemed. Then 16th,17th and modern theologians are consulted as to their particular requirements of specific types of redemption.

1.19. Sin and Redemption

According to Carol, in the 1955 issue of *Marian Studies* in the article, "Our Lady's Immunity From The Debt Of Sin," he states, "The theological background for our reflections will be furnished by the unique place which Our Lady occupies in the hierarchy of creation."[272] For Carol, there are three degrees or hierarchies of perfection[273] and Mary leads them all. The degrees or hierarchies of perfection for Carol are, "the order of nature, the order of grace, and the order of the Hypostatic Union."[274] For Carol he thinks all theologians are in agreement that Mary surpasses the orders of nature and grace since she is involved in the Incarnation.[275] Carol then quotes Italian Cardinal Cajetan, Master of the Dominican order, stating: "she alone, by her natural operation, touches the very limits of the Divinity."[276] Carol makes it clear that Mary isn't part of the Hypostatic Union, but he says, "But she belongs to the Hypostatic Order inasmuch as it was in her and through her that the Union was accomplished."[277] This necessitates the insistence for Carol to discuss the debt of sin. For Carol, we read that Mary is ontologically changed by her relationship with the Trinity and her role in the Hypostatic Order as he states, "The ineffable relationship established between Mary and the persons of the Adorable Trinity, as a result of the Hypostatic Union, imprints on her whole being a new, distinctive character, a unique rank which automatically raises her far above all choirs and

---

[272] Father Juniper Carol, O.F.M., "Our Lady's Immunity From The Debt Of Sin," *Marian Studies* 6 (1955): 165. (from now on cited as, Carol, Immunity).

[273] See Carol, Immunity, 165.

[274] See Carol, Immunity 165.

[275] See Carol, Immunity, 165.

[276] Carol, Immunity, 165.

[277] Carol, Immunity, 165.

hierarchies of creatures."[278] This association with her Son is necessary for understanding her predestination with him and her freedom from the debt of original sin. Carol says, "She stands in a category of her own, a category which far surpasses any and everything which is not God."[279]

In Carol's book, *Fundamentals of Mariology*, he explains the topic of Mary's immunity from actual sin in a methodical way. Firstly, Carol gives an analysis of the Catholic thesis (according to Carol), then secondly, he addresses errors in this area, and concludes with proofs of the doctrine from magisterial, biblical, and theological insights.[280]

Concerning Mary's immunity from actual sin the Catholic thesis, according to Carol in *Fundamentals* is this:

> The Blessed Virgin Mary, by a unique privilege
> of God, was preserved free from all actual sin
> during the entire course of her life. The meaning
> of this Catholic thesis is that Our Lady was never
> guilty of personal sin, either mortal or venial;
> that she was immune even from the slightest
> moral imperfections or willful violation or
> omission of any counsel of God or her superiors.
> Mary owes this privilege, not to her own merits,
> but to a singular favor of God.[281]

The reader is not given specifics about why this is the Catholic position, but could deduce from Carol's work *Fundamentals*, that it is the Magisterium, specifically Trent,

---

[278] Carol, Immunity, 165.
[279] Carol, Immunity, 165.
[280] See Carol, *Fundamentals*, 135.
[281] Carol, *Fundamentals*, 135.

Scripture, Tradition, and theological reason.[282] Nor are we given any clarity of Carol's thought on what the slightest moral imperfection of Mary's immunity could be. As general statement, I tend to agree with Carol. He refers the reader to Scheeben's second volume of *Mariology* for validation that all Mary has been privileged with is from God.[283]

The errors according to Carol in *Fundamentals* concern the denial of Mary's sinlessness by individuals such as Luther, Calvin, and other Protestants. Even some of the Fathers and ecclesiastical writers had comments in variance with the traditional Catholic position, such as St. Basil of Caesarea (St. Basil the Great fought against Arianism (329-379), and was bishop of Caesarea)[284] and even St. John Chrysostom (349-407, St. Chrysostom was a great speaker, known as the golden tongue, or mouth, was a monk and then bishop),[285] stated "when he claimed Mary's request for a miracle at the marriage feast of Cana was actually prompted by vainglory."[286]

Carol begins with a quote from the Council of Trent, (1547) in order to provide proofs from Catholic doctrine concerning Mary's immunity from actual sin. "If anyone shall say that man, after he is once justified, can avoid throughout his lifetime all sin, even venial, except by a special privilege of God, *as the Church holds concerning the Blessed Virgin*, let him be anathema."[287] Carol continues by referencing Pope Pius in 1567, "Pope Pius V proclaimed Our Lady's immunity from

---

[282] See, Carol, *Fundamentals*, 135.

[283] See Carol, *Fundamentals*, footnote 246., 135.

[284] See, Wikipedia, https://en.wikipedia.org/wiki/Basil_of_Caesarea

[285] See, FranciscanMedia.com, https://www.franciscanmedia.org/saint-john-chrysostom/

[286] Carol, *Fundamentals*,136.

[287] Carol, *Fundamentals*, 136. (Carol references DB, 833.) See, Council of Trent, Canon 23 on Justification.

personal sin by condemning one of Baius' propositions to the contrary. In 1854 Pius IX declared that Mary "was *always* free from *absolutely all* stain of sin." This coincides with the unqualified statement of Pius XII in his encyclical *Mystici Corporis* (1943) to the effect that Our Lady "was free from both *personal* and hereditary sin, and always most closely united with her Son."[288]

Arguments from the Bible for Mary's immunity from sin begin for Carol with Genesis 3:15. Carol emphasizes that an enmity such as this would exclude original and mortal sin. Concerning venial sin Carol says: "We know that venial sin does not destroy sanctifying grace (the friendship of God) in the soul; nevertheless, because it connotes a positive moral evil, it is quite incompatible with the absolute holiness which the Protoevangelium postulates for Our Blessed Lady."[289]

Finally, Carol looks at the arguments from Tradition for Mary's immunity from sin which he divides into three stages. The first argument looks at Mary's immunity from actual sin from the first five centuries, the second from the 5th to the 13th, and finally the 13th century until his day.

The first period of time from Tradition according to Carol for Mary's immunity from sin covers the first five centuries. Tradition speaks of an implicit reference to the Woman with her Son destroying the serpent and its seed.[290] Carol references St. Ephraem (declared Doctor of the Church in 1920, and composed over 400 hymns, some against heresies and some on virginity)[291] and St. Ambrose who both speak a bit

---

[288] Carol, *Fundamentals,* 137.

[289] Carol, *Fundamentals,* 138.

[290] See Carol, *Fundamentals*, 138.

[291] See, Wikipedia, https://en.wikipedia.org/wiki/Ephrem_the_Syrian

clearer on the topic, with Ambrose commenting: "Through grace the Virgin was free from all stain of sin."[292]

The next section of time, from the 5th until the 13th century, "Our Lady's sinlessness is never called into question, but is rather taken for granted by all."[293] From St. Augustine's statement: "We must except {sic}the Holy Virgin Mary, concerning whom—out of respect for the Lord—I wish to raise no question when dealing with sin."[294] Carol looks at Hildebert of Mans (1055-1133, French theologian, priest, and archbishop of Tours.)[295] and Walter of St. Victor (12th century philosopher and theologian who wrote around time of third Lateran Council (1179), was prior of monastery of St-Victor.)[296] who have a consistent emphasis in their writings concerning Mary's immunity from actual sin.

The third section Carol explores is the Scholastics. Carol writes, "the Scholastics not only taught that Mary had always been free from all actual or personal sin (whether mortal or venial), but they also began to discuss the causes—proximate and remote—of that sinlessness."[297] This brought up the question of whether Mary could sin. The matter of Mary's impeccability, or inability to sin are, according to Carol, looked at metaphysically and morally.[298] "The former is predicated exclusively of God who is holiness itself, and also of Christ, due to the Hypostatic Union. The latter belongs to the angels and saints on account of the beatific vision, and likewise to Our

---

[292] Carol, *Fundamentals*,138.

[293] Carol, *Fundamentals*, 139.

[294] Carol, *Fundamentals,* 139.

[295] See, Wikipedia, https://en.wikipedia.org/wiki/Hildebert

[296] See New Advent, http://www.newadvent.org/cathen/15544c.htm

[297] Carol, *Fundamentals,* 139.

[298] See Carol, *Fundamentals,* 140.

Blessed Lady, although for reasons other than those mentioned in the case of God, Christ, the angels and saints."[299] Top support this, Carol refers the reader to Alexander of Hales (d. 1245) who writes of Mary's impeccability due to the fullness of grace.[300] St. Bonaventure (d. 1274), according to Carol says Mary was the recipient of God's graces making it impossible for her to sin.[301] St. Thomas (d. 1274) "thought that Mary was impeccable owing to a constant act of divine Providence removing all occasions for sin from her path."[302] And Carol concludes by giving Suarez' opinion and many others who say that "the remote cause of Mary's impeccability was the divine Motherhood."[303] Carol says that for Suarez and others the proximate cause for Mary's impeccability had three reason: "The lack of concupiscence, the fullness of grace and an act of divine Providence which not only removed all occasions of sin from her but also confirmed her in grace."[304]

The final argument for Mary's immunity from actual sin are arguments from reason. For Carol, there are specific reasons for her to be sinless. The first is that "Mary was predestined from all eternity to be the *worthy* Mother of God. Any guilt of personal sin in her soul would naturally render her unworthy of so sublime a prerogative, for the shame of a parent rebounds to the disgrace of the child."[305] The second application of reason is that "Mary was chosen by God to be the Coredemptrix of mankind. And, as St. Bonaventure explains: "It is fitting that the Blessed Virgin, through whom the shame of sin was taken

---

[299] Carol, *Fundamentals*, 140.
[300] See Carol, *Fundamentals*, 140.
[301] See Carol, *Fundamentals*, 140.
[302] Carol, *Fundamentals*, 140.
[303] See Carol, *Fundamentals*, 140.
[304] Carol, *Fundamentals*, 140-141.
[305] Carol, *Fundamentals*, 141.

away, should so overcome the devil as never to be his victim.""[306]

Finally, Carol says that she is immune from actual sin because of her Queenship over all creation. The book, *Fundamentals* came out in 1956 and Mary's title as Queen of Heaven was officially given by Pope Pius XII., on October 11, 1954.[307] Carol writes,

> But how could the Queen require her subjects to observe the laws of God if she herself had failed therein? Therefore, we must assume that, since God had freely chosen Mary for all the above offices, He owed it to Himself to bestow the grace of sinlessness and impeccability upon her soul.[308]

What we realize is that Carol's arguments for Mary's immunity from actual sin are ones that he shares rather than ones that he personally develops as his own. Carol is not developing doctrine; rather, he is gathering sources and showing their historical development.

Father Carol says this about the *debitum pecati*:

(It is) the universal necessity to contract sin. 'This necessity is said to arise from two factors: (a) being conceived according to the normal laws of propagation; and (b) being included, by divine disposition, in the act of disobedience by which Adam lost the grace of God for all his

---

[306] Carol, *Fundamentals*, 141.

[307] See, *Ad caeli reginam*.

[308] Carol, *Fundamentals*, 141.

descendants. The former factor is supposed to
induce a remote necessity (debitum remotum) to
incur original sin; while the latter factor gives
rise to a proximate necessity (debitum
proximum) to contract it.'[309]

In this debate there are three varying opinions Carol has
noticed within this Marian field which need to be pointed out.
Carol writes:

> Some say that, since Mary was conceived by way
> of seminal generation, and since she was
> included in the will of Adam as the moral
> representative of the race, she should have
> contracted original sin, although, in fact, God
> suspended the application of the law in her case
> (here is the debitum proximum). 'Others claim
> that, owing to her normal generation, Mary
> should have been included in the sinful will of
> Adam, but God exempted her from this, and
> hence from actually contracting original sin
> (debitum remoter). 'A third group contends that
> God preserved Mary from every necessity
> (proximate or remote) to contract original sin.'[310]

---

[309] Rev. Juniper Carol, O.F.M. *A History of the Controversy Over the "Debitum Peccati."* in *Franciscan Institute Publications;* Theology Series No. 9, ed. George Marcil, O.F.M. (Bonaventure, NY, The Franciscan Institute of St. Bonaventure University, 1978), 12.

[310] Carol, *A History of the Controversy Over the "Debitum Peccati."* 4. He continues to state that many theologians consider this untenable because, "Mary was a true child of Adam by way of seminal generation; and it withholds her from the influence of Christ's redemption." 4,5. Replying to these arguments they say, "Seminal generation does not, of itself, create in the offspring a true *necessity* to contract original sin; it merely gives rise to a *possibility* of contracting it." Also pointed out, is we would inherit Adams and our ancestors sins if generation caused the transmission of sins. Ibid. Pg. 5. Finally, "For a person to be affected

127

The redemption of Mary is more beautiful and most perfect. All of these graces are the fruits of Jesus' redemptive work and its application to Our Lady before the Passion, for her calling as Mother of God. Carol writes in his book, *A History of the Controversy Over the "Debitum Peccati."*, about Mary's redemption, "The efficacy of the Savior's redemptive grace was so overwhelming in her case, that it not only preserved her from the actual contraction of sin, but even places her *beyond any possible reach* of the universal law of sin."[311]

Carol addresses this unique Marian teaching concerning her preservative redemption in the 1979 edition of *Marian Studies*. The article, "Reflections on the Problem of Mary's Preservative Redemption," is almost seventy pages in length and carefully examines the question of Mary's singular prerogative in the work of theologians before the definition of the Immaculate Conception up to the present.

In the Apostolic Constitution of Pius IX, *Ineffabilis Deus*, we read:

> We declare, pronounce, and define that the
> doctrine which holds that the most Blessed
> Virgin Mary, in the first instant of her
> conception, by a singular grace and privilege
> granted by Almighty God, in view of the merits
> of Jesus Christ, the Savior of the human race,
> was preserved free from all stain of original sin,
> is a doctrine revealed by God and therefore to be

---

by Adam's sin, a second factor is strictly necessary, namely, a decree of God withdrawing His grace from that individual whose solidarity with Adam in the *supernatural* order had been foreseen. Briefly, a true debt of sin presupposes that a person depends on the physical *and moral* headship of Adam. Now, Mary did not depend on Adam for her grace. It was the other way around." 5.

[311] Carol, *A History of the Controversy Over the "Debitum Peccati."* 5.

believed firmly and constantly by all the
faithful.[312]

Before unpacking the various theological questions
about Mary's preservative redemption Father Carol states what
is already held as *de fide* as well as that which the Church has
not defined. The following according to Carol are what the
Church has already defined:

1. that Our Lady was immune from all stain of original sin;
2. that this immunity coincided with the first instant of her
   conception;
3. that this immunity was due to a singular grace and
   privilege of Almighty God;
4. that this immunity was by way of preservation;
5. that Our Lady was redeemed by Christ.[313]

Carol then points out eight things that the Church has not
defined concerning Mary's preservative redemption:

1. the nature of original sin from which Mary was immune;
2. that the expression "*all* stain" includes immunity from the
   infectio carnis, or from the *debitum peccati*, or from
   concupiscence;
3. that the word 'singular' is to be understood in the sense
   of *exclusive*;
4. that the word 'grace' is to be understood of sanctifying
   grace and not of a divine, gratuitous favor;
5. that the word *privilege* is to be understood in the sense of
   a *dispensation* instead of an *exemption* from the law;

---

[312] Pope Pius IX, *Ineffabilis Deus*, (Boston, MA, St. Paul Books and Media), 21.

[313] Father Juniper Carol, O.F.M., "Reflections on the Problem of Mary's
Preservative Redemption." *Marian Studies* 30 (1979): 21. (Henceforth cited as
Carol, Reflections.).

6. that the merits of Christ were foreseen post *praevisum lapsum*;

7. that Christ redeemed Mary per modum redemptionis (reduplicative), per modum satisfactionis, and per modum sacrificii;

8. that the word *revealed* is to be understood in the sense of *formal* (explicit or implicit) instead of *virtual* revelation[314]

Father Carol's work in the 1979 *Marian Studies*, article "Reflections on the Problem of Mary's Preservative Redemption." continues by looking at some 17th century figures contributing to the doctrinal development of Mary's preservative redemption. He quotes a Jesuit named Augustine Bernal (d. 1642):

> (Augustine Bernal) openly taught that, since Our Lady had always been immune from original sin and even from the necessity to contract it, she could not have been redeemed by Christ. According to the author, we may say that Mary was redeemed in the sense that she was preserved from the *actual* sins she could have committed during her life.[315]

Carol also quotes Peter of St. John (d. 1684) a Carmelite who held that "Mary was predestined to be Christ's partner in the work of redeeming others. She was not freed from sin because she did not have any; she was not even preserved, since she *could not* have incurred original sin."[316] Carol carefully follows this Marian prerogative after the definition of the

---

[314] Carol, Reflections. 21–22.
[315] Carol, Reflections. 24.
[316] Carol, Reflections. 24.

Immaculate Conception. Looking at all of the variables offered from this theological contribution, Carol wishes to document the history of the teaching surrounding Mary's preservative redemption. He is not advancing a personal Marian perspective; rather, Carol synthesizes the work done thus far, in as thorough and organized manner as possible. He will even clarify the different ways theologians use the same words, such as "*redemptio sensu proprio*," when he says,

> For those who denied the Immaculate Conception, it was equivalent to "*redemptio sensu univoco.*" Which explains why many of them, with unassailable logic, regarded a preservative redemption as a contradiction in terms. As for St. Thomas, it is clear that "*redemptio proprie dicta*" meant a "liberation from sin already incurred," as Father Llamera has reminded us. And this position had its advocates as late as the 17th century, in spite of the explicitly pronouncement of Pope Sixtus IV to the contrary.[317]

The publication continues by looking at modern theologians and four areas of emphasis.

> "(a) To be redeemed '*sensu proprio*' Mary needed a *debitum proximum.* (b) To be redeemed '*sensu proprio*' Mary needed a *debitum conditionatum.* (c) To be redeemed '*sensu proprio*' Mary needed only a *debitum naturale.*

---

[317] Carol, "Reflections on the Problem of Mary's Preservative Redemption." 29.

(d) To be redeemed '*sensu proprio*' Mary needed no *debitum* at all.[318]

The work also looks at, The "Scientia Media" Solution, Scotus and his Marian impact, St. Thomas, and Bonnefoy. Carol concludes by restating:

> In this essay we have briefly stated our position on what is dogmatic and non-dogmatic in the 1854 definition of the Immaculate Conception. We have also discussed the various opinions of theologians on whether Our Lady was redeemed *sensu proprio* or rather *sensu improprio*. We have, moreover, sketched several of the theological attempts to harmonize Mary's preservative redemption with her immunity from the debt of sin.[319]

He ends the article with: "We believe that Our Blessed Lady was truly redeemed by the Passion of her Son and at the same time totally immune from the necessity to contract original sin."[320]

Considering the Incarnation of the Second Person of the Blessed Trinity, we may ask what role the Blessed Mother played in this event. Mary is not under the moral headship of Adam and has always been aligned with Christ's salvific mission and at enmity with the serpent.

Mary, then, had no obligation whatsoever to be in any way affected by the universal law of sin

---

[318] Carol, Reflections. 29.
[319] Carol, Reflections. 88.
[320] Carol, Reflections. 88.

which threatens every child of Adam even before he begins to exist. She was never under any debitum peccati of any kind, whether proximate or remote, personal or natural, absolute or conditional. She was, of course, a natural child of Adam. But, before she was predestined to be a child of Adam, she was already the object of God's ineffable love and affection.[321]

She is filled with grace,[322] being deprived of nothing, instead overflowing with life.[323] Mary, unlike Adam, yet like Christ, offers her life (the sword pierces her heart) for the Church. She fulfills what Eve should have done, in terms of obedience to the will of God.

Mary is blessed among women,[324] the masterpiece of creation, Immaculate with greater grace than the preternatural gifts given our first parents. If the Incarnation is not dependent upon Adam's sin, then Our Lady's role, even if not participating with Him as Coredemptrix, would still be so identified with Him, that our response to her should be *hyper-dulia*. The Incarnation is the greatest demonstration of God's love for humanity, and concerning matters of Jesus' Incarnation and mission, one always finds the Blessed Mary. For Carol, his concern is not so much the hypothetical question of Jesus' Incarnation based on Adam sinning or not sinning; rather, care

---

[321] Juniper, B. Carol, "Our Lady's Immunity from the Debt of Sin", *Marian Studies*, 6 (1955): 166–67.

[322] See, Luke 1:28.

[323] Father Carol says, "In our opinion, what Our Blessed Lady should have at her conception is grace, not original sin. Not that she had an antecedent right to it, of course; rather, since God had predestined her to the ineffable dignity of the divine motherhood, He owed it to Himself to grant her this unique privilege." A History of the controversy over the "Debitum Peccati," 6.

[324] See, Luke 1:42.

must be taken in examining the ramifications of Christ's primacy, regardless of sin.

In Jessica Kozack's thesis, concerning Carol's understanding of the *debitum peccati* she says: "The concept of the *debitum peccati* flows from the Franciscan idea of Mary's predestination due to her union with Christ."[325]

In light of the predestination of Mary with Jesus, original sin and its impact is different when considering its possible impact on Mary. Kozack writes:

> "To say that Mary has no *debitum* means that when ordaining the Immaculate Conception, God did not simply preserve Mary from "a sin she *should* have contracted...but rather from a sin she *would* have contracted, had God so decided [Carol's emphasis]." This thesis further removes Mary from sin by arguing that in the Immaculate Conception, God did not merely intercede to prevent Mary from obtaining Original Sin at the moment of conception; rather, He had always determined that she would not have this stain because she was predestined with Christ before the Fall. This means that she has no "debt to sin" because in no way was she ever under the obligation to contract Original Sin. This position is a corollary of Carol's understanding of Mary's association with Christ in the Hypostatic Order, as both are based on the presupposition that Mary was predestined with Christ in the same degree. At this point, Carol supports this aspect

---

[325] Kozack, *The Primacy of Christ as the Foundation of the Co-redemption*, 27.

of the Franciscan thesis simply by referring the definition of the Immaculate Conception in *Ineffabilis Deus* and the definition of the Assumption in *Munificentissimus Deus*, as "Both state unequivocally that Jesus and Mary were predestined 'uno eodemque decreto [one and the same decree].'"[326]

I do agree with Kozack's analysis of Carol's understanding of the *debitum*, but Carol is careful to explain the reasons why he holds to a particular line of thought. In Carol's 1977 article in *Marian Studies*, "The Blessed Virgin and the 'Debitum Peccati.' A Bibliographical Conspectus", Carol defines the *debitum* and addresses four responses to the understanding of the universal necessity to contract original sin concerning Mary. Then Carol provides a chronological bibliography of 564 theologians differentiating their opinions of the *debitum* by using eleven specific criteria. Concerning the *Debitum*, Carol uses the weight of these supporters, predominantly Franciscan but also from other orders, to prove why the Franciscan perspective is more fitting. Kozack says that Carol's emphasis on the *debitum peccati* is because, as some theologians say, he is out of touch:

> After the Council, Carol was never quite successful at directly engaging post-Conciliar theological trends. By 1975, his scholarly focus had shifted from the Coredemption to the debate over Mary's debitum peccati and preservative redemption. His position on these topics was "but the corollary of the absolute primacy of Christ." Thus, it is unsurprising that this work led

---

[326] Kozack, *The Primacy of Christ as the Foundation of the Co-redemption*, 27,28.

him to the publication of Why Jesus Christ?:
Thomistic, Scotistic and Conciliatory
Perspectives in 1986. In this work, Carol
defended the Franciscan thesis of Christ's
primacy and briefly offered his own conclusions
on this topic. Whereas before the Council Carol's
work was influential, many reviewers considered
this work out-of-touch with contemporary
theology.[327]

I think that this conclusion fair. If you look at the early
publication in *Marian Studies* (1955) and *Fundamentals* (1956),
and then compare it to works published in the late seventies,
such as *A History of the Controversy over the "debitum
peccati"* (1978) and his book *Why Jesus Christ?* (1986), he
treats the topic of the *debitum peccati* the same, with the later
publications unpacking his position even more thoroughly.
While Carol continues to remain consistent in his presentation
of the topics of the *debitum* and the predestination of Mary, it
seems to be less relevant, according to Kozack's argument that
theologians consider Carol to be out of touch. It seems to me
that Carol is locked into one area of thought that doesn't change
even after the Second Vatican Council.

Carol's Publications:

1955

"Our Lady's Immunity from the Debt of Sin," *Marian Studies* 6
(1955): 164–168. (This article looks at Mary's Immunity from
the debt of sin by looking at Mary's unique place in the

---

[327] Kozack, *The Primacy of Christ as the Foundation of the Co-redemption*, 11.

hierarchy of creation. She belongs to the Hypostatic Order,[328] according to Carol, and is not subject to the debt of sin because of her predestination with Christ.).

1956

Fundamentals of Mariology (New York, Benziger, 1956), xx, 1–203. This is a book providing the primary fundamentals of Mariology Carol taught which would teach seminarians, religious and priests. It is referenced here because of his treatment of the *Debitum Peccati* in the chapter, "Mary's Immunity from Actual Sin," 135-141.

1977

"The Blessed Virgin and the "Debitum Peccati." A Bibliographical Conspectus," *Marian Studies* 28 (1977), 181–256. This publication defines the *debitum* and addresses four responses to the understanding of the universal necessity to contract original sin concerning Mary. Then Carol provides a chronological bibliography of 564 theologians differentiating their opinions of the *debitum* by using eleven specific criteria.

1978

A History of the Controversy over the "Debitum Peccati", Franciscan Institute Publications. Theology Series, No. 9 (St. Bonaventure, NY.: The Franciscan Institute, 1978), xiii, 1–260. This book examines the topic of the *debitum* from the beginning (Augustine quoted for Carol's start point) and looks at primary religious figures who wrote on the topic. From Franciscans to

---

[328] "But she belongs to the Hypostatic Order inasmuch as it was in her and through her that the Union was accomplished." Carol, Immunity, 165.

Jesuits, key periods of debate and times of decline Carol explores the history of this controversy.

1979

"Reflections on the Problem of Mary's Preservative Redemption," *Marian Studies* 30 (1979): 19–88. This work looks at the teaching that denies Mary's redemption before the definition of the Immaculate Conception and after, and then the teaching that says Mary was redeemed. Then 16th, 17th and modern theologians are consulted as to their particular requirements of specific types of redemption.

COREDEMPTION

Fr. Juniper Home from Rome -- and Glad

Having looked at the predestination of Mary (publications spanning 1956-1986) and her immunity from the debt of sin (*Debitum Peccati*) (publications spanning 1955-1979), it is important to remember Carol's opinion on the two:

> "In our opinion, what Our Blessed Lady *should* have at her conception is grace, not original sin. Not that she had a right to it, of course; rather, since God had predestined her to the ineffable dignity of the divine motherhood (either *ante* or *post praevisum lapsum,* (before or after the fall) it matters not), He owed it to himself to grant her this unique privilege."[329]

This favor given Mary from God applies to her title and role as Coredemptrix[330]

Carol's publications on Mary as Coredemptrix are numerous especially in his early years of study.

> "From 1936 to 1950, he wrote some twenty-five articles on Mary's coredemption, publishing them in various periodicals, particularly in the Marianum which was just begun by the Servites

---

[329] "The Blessed Virgin and the 'Debitum Peccati.' A Bibliographical Conspectus", *Marian Studies* 28 (1977): 185, footnote 11.

[330] "From 1937 to 1940, he pursued his theological studies at the Pontifical Antonianum in Rome and prepared a doctoral dissertation on Mary's co-redemption." *Marianum* (1991), 710.

in Rome in 1939. He had an article there already in the second issue (fasc. II, 1939)."[331]

In Carol's book, *Fundamentals of Mariology* he writes:

> Our Blessed Lady does not produce directly and physically the sanctifying grace given to us through the Sacraments, nevertheless, she intervenes in that production in a twofold manner. First, remotely, inasmuch as that sacramental grace was merited by her (together with Christ) as Coredemptrix while she was on earth. Secondly, proximately (although indirectly), inasmuch as the very desire to receive the Sacraments, and the proper dispositions to do so worthily are the effect of actual graces which are granted to the recipient in each case through the intercession of Our Blessed Lady.[332]

As with the previous two chapters, so too here will be given a brief annotated bibliography of the primary sources we will look at in this fifth chapter:[333]

1936

"In Defense of the Title of Coredemprix," *Homiletic and Pastoral Review* 36 (1936): 1197–99. An article defending the legitimacy of the use of the title of Mary as Cordemptrix. He specifically responds to the then recent views of Father Albert

---

[331] Koehler, "In Homage to the Founder of the Mariological Society of America," 710.

[332] Carol, *Fundamentals*, 71.

[333] At the end of the chapter will be a list of Carol's publications dealing with this topic.

F. Kaiser, C.PP.S in the June issue of *Homiletic and Pastoral Review*. He addresses the concerns that the term is wrong and erroneous.

1937

"The Holy See and the Title of 'Co-redemptrix'," *Homiletic and Pastoral Review* 37 (1937): 746–48. This article is a response to the editors of *Homiletic and Pastoral Review* for a comment by an unnamed reader who said the title of Coredemtrix used by Carol concerning Mary was erroneous. Carol makes it clear that the doctrine of her coredemption can be expressed even if the term isn't used (p.747).

1943

"Our Lady's Part in the Redemption According to Seventeenth-century writers," *Franciscan Studies* 24 (1943): 3–20; 143–58. This article looks at Mary's part in redemption from the theologians and Catholic writers of the seventeenth-century. Carol concludes by stating that Our Lady's part of the objective work of redemption is not a recent invention.

1956

Fundamentals of Mariology (New York, Benziger, 1956), xx, 1–203. This is a book providing the primary fundamentals of Mariology Carol taught which would teach seminarians, religious and priests. It is referenced here because of his treatment of Mary as Coredemptrix of mankind. Carol says more important than the word Coredemptrix is the doctrine conveyed by the word. He looks at six points to address this.

1957

"Our Lady's Co-redemption," in *Mariology*, ed. J. B. Carol, (Milwaukee: Bruce Pub. Co., 1957), 2: 377–425. This article looks at Mary's position in the economy of salvation (see P. 377), and her cooperation with Jesus, in a mediately and immediately way (P. 379). He looks at the Ordinary Magisterium, the teaching of Tradition, nature and modalities of her coredemption and looks at difficulties and solutions.

Having examined Our Lady's predestination with the primacy of Christ, as well as her preservation from sin through a more sublime redemption. We now address her earthly identification with Jesus as Coredemptrix (Carol's publications span the longest period of time of the three Marian themes we have looked at; 1936-1978). While any emphasis on Mary as Coredemtrix may seem to be problematic when promoting the salvific work of Jesus to those of a non-Catholic background, Carol insisted that we not forget her role, having been chosen by God in such a singular way. She will assist us not only in battling misunderstandings and heresies, but also in pouring out the graces of her Son. In Carol's third volume of *Mariology* he realizes that while theological understanding of Mary is difficult for many outside of the Catholic faith, she is key in reuniting all into the faith. He says,

> For it is precisely in this area that we encounter some of the stumbling blocks which allegedly retard the much-hoped-for return of our separated brethren to the source and center of doctrinal unity. Paradoxically, it is also in this very area that the hope of reunion lies. If Our Blessed Lady is properly styled the "Destroyer of All Heresies" and the "Channel of All Graces,"

then it stands to reason that the cult of which she
is the object cannot but exert a profoundly
beneficial influence on the complex and delicate
process of reuniting all God's children into the
one fold of salvation.[334]

For Carol, the hope of uniting the separated brethren back into
unity rests in a deeper understanding of Mary.

An example of striving to clarify Mary's Coredemptive
role with people of differing Marian views is found in Father
Carol's written account dealing with Father Kaiser, a theologian
holding to a different perspective on Mary's title as
Coredemptrix. Carol addressed some of these Marian concerns
in his article "The Holy See and the Title of Coredemptrix" that
appeared in the 1937 issue of *The Homiletic and Pastoral
Review*, where he argues that he is:

> "Overjoyed to hear that the writer sincerely
> regrets having thoughtlessly stated that the title
> of "Coredemptrix" was a novelty, erroneous and
> smacking of heathenism. I am also glad to see
> that, even in his opinion, this title might be said
> to be apt, and "must be said to be theologically
> sound and legitimate." Fr. Kaiser likewise admits
> that the mere prefix "co" does not necessarily
> carry the connotation of equality even in other
> English or German words. So far, we are in
> perfect agreement.[335]

---

[334] Carol, *Mariology* 3, viii.

[335] Father Juniper B. Carol, O.F.M., "The Holy See and the Title of "Co-redemptrix.", *The Homiletic and Pastoral Review,* (New York, NY; J.F. Wagner, 1937), 746.

There are some areas though in which the two priests are clearly not in agreement and Father Carol begins straightaway to address these differences. Father Kaiser must have attempted to state that Carol insisted that the word Coredemptrix was indispensable and that the use of this teaching of Mary as Coredemptrix would be of greater importance if Rome had used it within a Latin context. Carol responds:

> At no time did I state that the title of "Coredemptrix" was *indispensable* in the declaration of the Catholic doctrine of Mary's association with Christ in the Redemption. Hence, much of what Fr. Kaiser has in his communication is not to the point. All I contended was that, as a matter of fact, Rome *does* style our Blessed Mother "Coredemptrix" of the human race, not merely once but on repeated occasions?[336]

The matter raised by Father Kaiser concerning the difficulty of explaining the term Coredemptrix is next dealt with by Father Carol in the same article, where Carol says:

> The writer tells us the term "Coredemptrix" needs an explanation, at least for the non-Catholic mind and for the ill-informed Catholic, so as to avoid possible erroneous implications. Well and good; but I maintain that the fact that it should be explained to the unlearned is no reason why we should avoid its use. Do not the terms "infallibility" and "mother of God," for instance, demand an accurate explanation and even a

---

[336] Carol, "The Holy See and the Title of "Co-redemptrix.", 746.

marked restriction? Yet, who would think of avoiding their use simply on that score? Protestants have, as a rule, misinterpreted these and hundreds of other Catholic terms; why not avoid them all in order to be consistent?" Carol then says: "And I also wish to state that one may aptly express the doctrine of Coredemption without using the very word "Coredemptrix." Thus, Pope Benedict XV says that Mary redeemed the human race with Christ, and yet does not employ the term "Coredemptrix." The present Pope, however, while approving of Benedict XV's terminology, chooses rather the word "Coredemptrix" itself on no less than two occasions (*Osservatore Romano,* March 25, 1934; *ibid.,* April 29-30,1935).[337]

Father Carol finishes his response to Father Kaiser's arguments by dealing with the false idea from Kaiser that Carol stated the term Coredemptrix was "*generally* accepted in the thirteenth century."[338] Carol insisted that he did not say that, but rather, says:

I simply stated that around the year 1300 Alanus Veranius speaks of it not as something new or composed by himself, but as something which was already generally accepted. In other words, it is Alanus who gives that impression in his writings, not I. Personally, I do not think that this title was in *general* use at the time of Sts. Bonaventure, Thomas, and Albertus Magnus.

---

337 Carol, "The Holy See and the Title of "Co-redemptrix.", 747.
338 Carol, "The Holy See and the Title of "Co-redemptrix.", 747.

The learned Scotus did know of it at least in its simpler form, namely, "Redemptrix" (cFr. *Lib. Sent.* and *Report. Paris.*, III, Dist. III, q.i). Besides, does it make any difference whether or not it was generally used in the thirteenth century? May not the Church at any time approve of any terminology she deems fit to express a given doctrine?[339]

Father Kaiser's last argument that Carol argues against was that the Holy See does not infallibly state that Mary is "Coredemptrix". Carol writes:

Very true; but he will agree with us that it is not the task of any private theologian to "check up" on the wording of Papal documents. These although not infallible, are always very carefully drawn up and deserve our respect. If the Holy See does not care to avoid the use of the title of "Co-redemptrix," but has repeatedly inserted it in its Decrees, why should Fr. Kaiser insist that it should be avoided? Shall we doubt that the wisdom and prudence of the Holy See far exceed ours?[340]

With this published response to Father Kaiser, Carol addresses quite decisively many of the arguments people still emphasize today concerning the title of Mary as Coredemptrix. It is a difficult term needing clear explanation to the un-catechized and to the non-Catholic, but we must be lucid in our teaching regardless the audience. While the Church has not at

---

[339] Carol, "The Holy See and the Title of "Co-redemptrix.", 747.
[340] Carol, "The Holy See and the Title of "Co-redemptrix." 748.

this time dogmatically declared the term Coredemptrix to be used in speaking of Mary's role in the redemptive work of her son, it certainly has been used in this way, along with many clergy and saints as Carol demonstrated. "And, as a matter of fact, the title of *Coredemptrix* has come into general use in modern times and counts in its favor not only the Holy See (which would be sufficient) but an endless host of Cardinals, bishops, theologians and Catholic writers of renown."[341]

This term of Coredemption is a bit more developed from the 1937 article in *Homiletic and Pastoral Review*, in his 1956 book *Fundamentals of Mariology*. We will see that Carol still finds it important to argue opposing opinions at odds with the title Coredemptix, but in this book those arguments are more general and not directed to any one person.

In 1956, Carol's book *Fundamentals of Mariology* gives some of the basic teachings he would present to seminarians and religious in the field of Marian studies. One such topic he taught on was Mary as Coredemptrix. Carol places the work of Mary as Coredemptrix, with and under her Son, in the fifth chapter of *Fundamentals*, which deals with Mary's universal mediation. He says:

> It is correct to say that Mary is our spiritual
> Mother *because* she is our Mediatrix, and also
> that she is our Mediatrix *because* she is our
> spiritual Mother. When applied to Our Blessed
> Lady the term "Mediatrix" designates a twofold
> function: first, reconciling mankind with God
> through her cooperation in the redemptive work
> of Christ while she was still on earth; second,

---

[341] Carol, "The Holy See and the Title of "Co-redemptrix." 747.

making available to each individual soul the graces which were earned by Christ and by herself through the work of Redemption. The first phase of her Mediation was accomplished on Calvary; the second is being constantly carried out and will continue until the end of the world.[342]

Carol unpacks the teaching about Coredemption by emphasizing that since at least the 15th century Mary has been called "Coredemptrix."[343] With the rich heritage of this teaching, along with Catholic hierarchy and papal writings Carol emphasizes, "Hence its legitimacy is now beyond question. But more important than the word *Coredemtprix* itself, is the doctrine conveyed by that word."[344]

There are six primary points Carol will emphasize amidst the varying opinions concerning this teaching of Mary as Coredemptrix. The first addresses, "the meaning of Redemption and Coredemption" the second, "various opinions concerning Mary's Coredemption;" the third, "the teaching of the magisterium;" the fourth, "the argument of Sacred Scripture;" the fifth, "the teaching of Tradition;" and the sixth, "objections against the doctrine."[345] These six points lay a foundation for Carol's reasoning that the word Coredemptrix is legitimate, as is the doctrine behind the word.[346]

---

[342] Carol, *Fundamentals*, 55–6.

[343] Carol, *Fundamentals*, 56.

[344] Carol, *Fundamentals*, 57.

[345] Carol, *Fundamentals*, 57.

[346] See Carol, *Fundamentals*, 57.

For the first area of emphasis of Mary as Coredemptrix, Carol states:

> In Catholic theology the term "Redemption" designates the sum total of meritorious and satisfactory acts performed by Christ while on earth, offered to the eternal Father in and through the sacrifice of the cross, in virtue of which the eternal Father was moved (humanly speaking) to reinstate the human race into His former friendship. Accordingly, when we say that Our Lady is the "Coredemptrix" of mankind, we mean that, together with Christ (although subordinately to Him and in virtue of His power) she atoned or satisfied for our sins, merited every grace necessary for salvation, and offered her divine Son on Calvary to appease the wrath of God, and that, as a result of this, God was pleased to cancel our debt and receive us into His former friendship. This coredemptive role of Mary actually began when she, out of her own free will, made possible the coming of the Redeemer into the world by accepting to become His Mother.[347]

In this first point Mary offers the world its Savior by being the Mother of our Redeemer (mediately (indirectly, remotely)[348] or remotely (directly, proximately) according to

---

[347] Carol, *Fundamentals*, 57–8.

[348] See "Our Lady's Coredemption." *Mariology*, ed. J. B. Carol O.F.M., vol. 2, Milwaukee, Bruce Pub. Co., 1957. 379.

Carol),[349] and she offers her suffering with Christ at Calvary (immediately or proximately according to Carol).[350]

In the second point, Carol addresses the varying opinions regarding Mary's Coredemption specifically found in non-Catholics, who do not believe Mary can be called Coredemptrix,[351] and certain theologians who emphasize "that Mary's cooperation, while formal, was nevertheless only remote or mediate."[352]

Third, Carol looks at the teaching of the Magisterium using the term Coredemptrix along with its doctrine, acknowledging that the Church has not definitively settled this matter. Here he quotes Benedict XV's Apostolic Letter *Inter Sodalicia* (March 22,1918), which says, "To such extent did she (Mary) suffer and almost die with her suffering and dying Son, and to such extent did she surrender her maternal rights over her Son for man's salvation, and immolated Him, insofar as she could, in order to appease the justice of God, that *we may rightly say that she redeemed the human race together with Christ.*"[353] Father Carol references Pius XI who in a radio interview referred to Mary as Coredemptrix, and that the pope "called Our Lady *Coredemptrix* on at least five other occasions."[354] For Carol, the reference by the Catholic hierarchy, writers and even papal documents[355]makes the term

---

349 See Carol, *Fundamentals*, 58.
350 See Carol, *Fundamentals*, 58.
351 See Carol, *Fundamentals*, 58.
352 Carol, *Fundamentals*, 59.
353 Carol, *Fundamentals*, 59–60.
354 Carol, *Fundamentals*, 60.
355 See Carol, *Fundamentals*, 56-57.

Coredemptrix unquestionably valid, as he says, "Hence its legitimacy is now beyond question."[356]

The fourth point looks at Sacred Scripture and its application to Mary as Coredemptrix. While the Bible does not overtly use the word Coredemptrix, Carol makes mention of the Genesis 3:15, which he calls the Protoevangelium.[357] The primary scriptural reference for Coredemption according to Carol remains to be found in Genesis the third chapter, fifteenth verse, where we are given, according to his use of the word,[358] the Protoevangelium, meaning the first Messianic prophesy. The verse reads, "I will put enmity between you and the woman, and between your offspring and hers; he will strike at your head, while you strike at his heel."[359] For Carol, "The crushing of the serpent's head is, of course, a figure of speech used here to describe the work of Redemption which will utterly destroy the devil's power over men."[360] According to Carol this verse foreshadows Mary as Coredemptrix because we see she shares the same victory over Satan as Christ.[361] This association with the Woman and her seed in complete opposition to the serpent is foundational according to Carol for understanding Mary as Mediatrix and Coredemptrix. As emphasized before, Carol states,

> When applied to Our Blessed Lady the term
> *Mediatrix* designates a twofold function: first,
> reconciling mankind with God through her

---

[356] Carol, *Fundamentals*, 57.

[357] See Carol, *Fundamentals*, 61.

[358] Carol, Fundamentals, 61.

[359] Genesis 3:15, *The Catholic Answer Bible, NAB.* (Wichita, KS, Fireside Catholic Publishing, Our Sunday Visitor, Inc. DeVore and Sons, Inc., 2002).

[360] Carol, *Fundamentals*, 61.

[361] See Carol, *Fundamentals*, 61,62.

cooperation in the redemptive work of Christ
while she was still on earth; second, making
available to each individual soul the graces
which were earned by Christ and by herself
through the work of Redemption." "In virtue of
the first function Mary is called *Coredemptrix*; in
virtue of the second: "Dispenser of all graces.[362]

Carol then makes mention of Luke 1:26-38 where
Mary's yes to the Incarnation is of great salvific importance. "In
a very true sense, then, God made the Redemption of the world
dependent upon Mary's consent; and she gave it knowingly and
willingly. This consent was undoubtedly ratified on Calvary
when she stood at the foot of the cross suffering with her Son
(Luke 2:35) and indeed for the selfsame purpose, namely the
reconciliation of God and man."[363]

In the fifth point Carol looks at concerning Mary as
Coredemptrix is the teaching of Tradition. Carol states that the
idea of his teaching of Mary as Coredemptrix "was already
contained in the ancient doctrine portraying her in the role of a
new and Second Eve."[364] Using a comparison of Eve and Mary,
starting with St. Justin Martyr and St. Irenaeus the developing
idea, or germ of the current understanding of Mary as
Coredemptrix was this:

> The essence of the antithesis lies in this, that just
> as Eve cooperated with Adam in the sin that
> doomed the whole race, so Mary has cooperated
> with Christ, the second Adam, in bringing about
> the rehabilitation of mankind lost by that sin; just

---

[362] Carol, *Fundamentals*, 56.

[363] Carol, *Fundamentals*, 62.

[364] Carol, *Fundamentals*, 62

as Eve, through her disobedience, had become the cause of death and damnation to her race, so Mary, through her acquiescence to God's will at the time of the Annunciation, had become the cause of life and salvation to mankind.[365]

This idea of Mary's cooperation with Christ developed to the point where in the 12th century, Arnold of Chartres (d. 1160) and his influence brought about more specifically the teaching of Mary as Coredemptris. Carols writes:

> "Thus, in the 12th century, and particularly under the influence of Arnold of Chartres (d. 1160), we begin to find frequent and specific allusions to the redemptive character of Our Lady's compassion and her oblation on Calvary. By the end of the 17th century, a large number of theologians and Catholic writers were already teaching the doctrine of Mary's Coredemption in exactly the same sense as we do today."[366]

For Carol, Chartres's influence is a noteworthy example in understanding Mary as Coredemptrix, in that she offers her suffering with Christ at Calvary.

Finally, for Carol in *Fundamentals*, he looks at three primary objections to the teaching of Mary as Coredemptrix. The first objection Carol addresses deals with is the argument that Christ is the only Mediator and Redeemer.[367] To this objection, Carol responds:

---

[365] Carol, *Fundamentals*, 62–63.
[366] Carol, *Fundamentals*, 63.
[367] Carol, *Fundamentals*, 65.

We have seen above that these same sources point to Our Blessed Lady as Christ's associate in the Redemption. Therefore, when they state that Christ alone is our Redeemer, they are obviously referring to the primary, universal and self-sufficient causality of Christ in the redemptive process. This does not exclude Mary's secondary and completely subordinate cooperation, which drew all its efficacy from the superabundant merits of her divine Son.[368]

The second objection Carol addresses concerning Mary's Coredemption argues that Mary cannot both receive and effect Redemption. "How could she, at one and the same time, receive the *effect* of the Redemption and be the *cause* of it?"[369] Carol responds:

> Mary cooperated to redeem others, not herself. Christ redeemed Mary first with a preservative Redemption, and then, together with her, He redeemed all others with a liberative Redemption. This does not, of course, correspond to two distinct Redemptions, but rather to a twofold intention on the part of Christ. This twofold intention, in turn, produced a twofold effect: one affecting Mary alone, and the other (with the cooperation of Mary) affecting the rest of mankind. Once Mary was redeemed by Christ (with a logical priority), she was able

---

[368] Carol, *Fundamentals*, 64.

[369] Carol, *Fundamentals*, 64.

to cooperate with Him in the Redemption of others.[370]

This argument is excellent in the articulation of the two points of intent and effect of the one Redemption.

The third argument for Mary's Coredemption argues that Jesus Christ's work and its satisfaction was infinite so how can this be enhanced by Mary?[371] Carol wraps up his Marian defense: "Our Lady's cooperation did not and could not enhance the value of Christ's redemptive acts. However, God was pleased to accept the former together with the latter merely as constituting a new title for our Redemption. Surely, God could have arranged things otherwise; but He chose to arrange them that way."[372] This argument does not negate God's ability to do something a different way; rather, it simply says He chose to do things in a way that was pleasing. For Carol, this argument is satisfied with God choosing to do something in a way that is simply reduced to His choice.

In 1957, one year after the publication of *Fundamentals of Mariology*, Father Carol wrote a chapter, "Our Lady's Coredemption" published in the second volume of *Mariology*. In this work, Carol writes in more depth about Mary as Coredemptrix, but we see many of the same arguments from *Fundamentals* repeated here. Just as he explained Mary's mediate and immediate cooperation in *Fundamentals*, so too in this chapter Carol emphasizes that point. Father Carol writes:

> There are two ways Mary cooperated in Christ's redemptive work: mediately (indirectly,

---

[370] Carol, *Fundamentals*, 64–65.

[371] See Carol, *Fundamentals*, 65.

[372] Carol, *Fundamentals*, 65.

remotely) and immediately (directly, proximately). Mary cooperated mediately, for example, by meriting some of the circumstances of the Incarnation, and chiefly by giving birth to the world's Savior. Since Mary knowingly and willingly consented to the coming of Christ with a view to man's Redemption, it is clear that this cooperation of hers was moral and formal, notwithstanding its being mediate. She cooperated immediately if her merits and satisfactions were accepted by Almighty God together with the merits and satisfactions of Christ to bring about the selfsame effect, namely, the restoration of the human race to God's former friendship. Another type of immediate cooperation would be had, for example, if Our Lady had determined Christ (by request, command, counsel, etc.) to perform the work of Redemption, thus directly influencing the Savior's redemptive acts in themselves.[373]

Mary's free consent to the coming of the Redeemer, along with uniting all prayers and sufferings to her Son are examples, according to Father Carol of Marian mediation that Catholic theologians acknowledge, although agreement varies when discussing the value, efficacy and extent of her collaboration.[374] So Carol will address a couple objections some theologians may have with Mary as Coredemptrix.

---

[373] "Our Lady's Coredemption." *Mariology*, ed. J. B. Carol O.F.M., vol. 2, Milwaukee, Bruce Pub. Co., 1957. 379. (cited from now on as "Our Lady's Coredemption", *Mariology 2*).

[374] See Carol, "Our Lady's Coredemption", *Mariology 2*, 379–80.

The first group says that Mary's association with Jesus as Redeemer had no value or efficacy for objective Redemption, but only in applying the fruits of Redemption to individual souls.[375] According to Carol, to this group Mary distributes the graces of Jesus' redemptive work. She earns the right to do so by her merits.[376]

Another group of theologians Carol says, hold to the position that Mary "cooperated proximately, directly and immediately, in the Redemption itself (*objective* Redemption) inasmuch as Almighty God was pleased to accept her merits and satisfactions together with those of Christ (although subordinately to them) as having redemptive value for the liberation of mankind from the slavery of Satan and its supernatural rehabilitation."[377] This latter position is what Carol held to and he applauded the efforts of J. Lebron, J. M. Bover, S.J., and others in articulating these distinctions.[378] Here Carol is clear that Mary as Coredeemer but it is different from Christ as Redeemer. Mary unites her merits and satisfactions with Christ, whereas Christ's merits and satisfactions were infinite and limitless.[379]

The third position that Carol articulates in the chapter, "Our Lady's Coredemption," was an attempt to be an option in between the previous two. Carol writes:

> Our Blessed Lord *alone* brought about our reconciliation with God *in actu primo*. This presupposed, Our Lady may be said to have

---

[375] See Carol, "Our Lady's Coredemption", *Mariology* 2, 380.

[376] See Carol, "Our Lady's Coredemption", *Mariology* 2, 380.

[377] Carol, "Our Lady's Coredemption", *Mariology* 2, 380.

[378] See Carol, "Our Lady's Coredemption", *Mariology* 2, 380.

[379] See Carol, "Our Lady's Coredemption", *Mariology* 2, 380.

proximately cooperated in the objective Redemption in the sense that she "accepted" the fruits of the Savior's redemptive sacrifice and made them available to the members of the Church whom she officially represented on Calvary.[380]

Father Carol did not think this was truly a middle course. He pointedly states, "While their advocates frequently use the terminology of the second group (a clever camouflage), actually their explanation (or destruction?) of Our Lady's Coredemption coincides substantially with that of professors Lennerz (Heinrich Lennerz, a Jesuit and professor at the Gregorian University in Rome while Lonergan was a student there.) and Goossens (Goossens is, according to Carol, a distinguished theologican that he is aligned with Lennerz, and G.D. Smith in connection to Mary's distribution of graces)."[381]

The teaching of Mary as Coredemptrix presented by Carol to seminarians and religious as published in *Fundamentals* is unpacked a bit more in depth in his chapter "Our Lady's Coredemption" in *Mariology 2*. Carol is not interested in creating new doctrine, simply developing and expanding the doctrine from the Magisterial, Scriptural and Traditional perspective.[382] Father Carol also unpacked and emphasized the difficulties of Coredemption in both *Fundamentals* and *Mariology 2*, expanding further these doctrinal oppositions in the second volume of *Mariology*.[383] In addition to identifying and answering the difficulties with Mary as Coredemptrix, both works look at the difficulty in reconciling

---

[380] See Carol, "Our Lady's Coredemption", *Mariology* 2, 381.

[381] See Carol, "Our Lady's Coredemption", *Mariology* 2, 381.

[382] See Carol, "Our Lady's Coredemption", *Mariology* 2, 382–409.

[383] See Carol, "Our Lady's Coredemption", *Mariology* 2, 416–424.

Christ as the one mediator and Mary as the secondary mediator, and the problem of the cause of merit not being the result or effect of merit.

The term Coredemptrix was and is unsettling to some theologians, as we have observed, yet Carol states that while this is the case, careful work must be done to articulate proper Marian doctrine. "It remains true that many dogmatic questions will not be satisfactorily solved nor properly understood until they are solved and understood through a well-focused prism of the fundamental doctrine relative to Our Lady's position in the economy of salvation."[384]

Father Juniper Carol defended the term of Mary as Coredemptrix so regularly because the title conveyed the doctrine of who she was and is. For Carol, this doctrine of Coredemption, while considered by many to be problematic, was a theological endeavor worth articulating. Carol wrote in 1957.

> Those who are fairly abreast of current Catholic thought scarcely need to be apprised of the importance attached to the problem of Our Lady's Coredemption in contemporary theological literature. They are aware of the fact that during the past twenty-five years particularly, few questions in the vast field of the sacred sciences have engaged the attention of theologians more frequently and absorbingly than the one we are about to discuss. Even the Protestant theologian Giovanni Miegge recognizes this truth when he maintains that

---

[384] Carol, "Our Lady's Coredemption", *Mariology* 2, 377.

Mary's Coredemption is the central and
fundamental issue in twentieth-century
Mariology.[385]

What is of importance, and worthy of reiterating is that
Father Carol does not insist that the term *Coredemptrix* be
indispensable. He finds it difficult to see why it not be utilized,
but the teaching itself is without question, even if the term is not
dogmatically declared.

A small aside worth mentioning is that Carol's
publications on Coredemption seem to be very minimal after
Vatican II. If publications are any example of where he focused
his attention, it would be the book, *Why Jesus Christ?,*
published in 1986. This book is the culmination of his previous
studies in the Scotistic and Thomistic perspectives concerning
the absolute primacy and predestination of Jesus Christ and
Mary his mother. This seems to be the Marian focus for Carol in
his publications after the Second Vatican Council.

Kozack notes that this lessening of emphasis on Mary as
Coredemptrix may be due to Vatican II calling Mary Mediatrix
and not Coredemptrix. Kozack writes:

> Carol notes that those who would limit Mary's
> mediation to the dispensation of grace argue that
> the Fathers call Mary *Mediatrix* not
> *Coredemptrix*. However, Carol argues that based
> on what he has shown, mediation includes much
> more than dispensing grace. Carol's opponents
> limited the term *Mediatrix* to indicating actual
> moral mediation, rather than including its

---

[385] Carol, "Our Lady's Coredemption", *Mariology* 2, 377.

ontological and radical moral components. Carol admits that the Fathers often use *Mediatrix* in the context of dispensing grace; however, they use it in many other contexts as well, citing as support Basil of Seleucia, Antipater of Bostra, and Sophronius of Jerusalem, who all discuss Mary's mediation in the context of the Redemption. Furthermore, Paul calls Christ the one Mediator in the context of the Redemption (1 Tim. 2:5-6). Overall, Carol holds that the term "mediation" has multiple meanings, including Redemption in our *post lapsum* state; therefore, Mary's title as *Mediatrix* indicates that she mediates in multiple ways, including Coredemption.[386]

This argument by Kozack though is based on the earlier works of Carol since there are not a lot of published works by him specifically on Coredemption after Vatican II. The inclusion of Coredemption in the title Mediatrix is not inconsistent with Carol but we have little to affirm Coredemption was his focus after the Council.

An annotated list of Carol's Publications on Coredemption is provided for further reading: (book reviews are simply offered for further review by interested parties).

1936

"In Defense of the Title of Coredemprix," *Homiletic and Pastoral Review* 36 (1936): 1197–99. An article defending the legitimacy of the use of the title of Mary as Cordemptrix. He specifically responds to the then recent views of Father Albert

---

[386] Kozack, *The Primacy of Christ as the Foundation of the Co-redemption*, 25-26.

F. Kaiser, C.PP.S in the June issue of *Homiletic and Pastoral Review*. He addresses the concerns that the term is wrong and erroneous.

1937

"The Theological Concept of Mediation and Co-redemption," *Ephemerides Theologicae Lovanienses* 14 (1937): 642–650. The importance of the theological concept of mediation and Coredemption.

"*The Blessed Virgin's Co-redemption Vindicated. Short Observations on a Recent Work*." (Quaracchi [Florence] 1937), pp. 30.

"The Holy See and the Title of 'Co-redemptrix'," *Homiletic and Pastoral Review* 37 (1937): 746–48. This article is a response to the editors of *Homiletic and Pastoral Review* for a comment by an unnamed reader who said the title of Coredemptrix used by Carol concerning Mary was erroneous. Carol makes it clear that the doctrine of her coredemption can be expressed even if the term isn't used (P. 747).

1939

"De fundamento proximo Co-redemptionis Marianae," The Immediate foundation of the Cordemption of Mary., *Marianum* 1 (1939):173–187.

"Utrum Beatae Virginis Coredemptio sit in S. Scriptura formaliter revelata," The Virgin's Cordemption, whether it is in Scripture, formally unveiled., *Marianum* 1 (1939): 283–326.

"The Nature of the Blessed Virgin's Ontological Mediation," *Miscellanea Francescana* 39 (1939): 449–470.

"Episcopatus catholicus et Beatae Virginis Co-redemptio," (Episcopate and the Virgin Coredemption)., *Ephemerides Theologicae Lovanienses* 10 (1939): 801–828.

Hermann Seiler., S.J*., Corredemptrix*, in *Marianum* 1 (1939): 237–40. (Book Review)

Hermann Seiler, S.J., *Corredemptrix*, in *Antonianum* 14 (1939): 412. (Book Review)

1940

"Pater H. Lennerz et problema de Co-redemptione Mariana," Father H. Lennerz and the problem of Marian Co-redemption., *Marianum* 2 (1940): 194–200.

"De Sanctorum Patrum Doctrina circa Beatae Virginis Corredemptionem," The doctrine of the Fathers about the Blessed Virgin's Coredemption, *Marianum* 2 (1940), pp. 256–66.

"Method in Mariology: An open letter to the Very Rev. Dr. Smith Concerning Mary's Co-redemption," *Clergy Review* 18 (1940): 371–75.

1941

Doctrina de Beatae Virginis Coredemptione ab ortu usque ad prolapsu, aetatis Scholasticorum, The doctrine of the Virgin's coredemption from the beginning to the end of the Scholastic period. *Miscellanea* Francescana 41 (1941): 248–66.

1943

"Our Lady's part in the Redemption according to Seventeenth-century writers," *Franciscan Studies* 24 (1943): 3–20; 143–58.

This article looks at Mary's part in redemption by the theologians and Catholic writers of the seventeenth century. Carol concludes by stating that Our Lady's part in the objective work of redemption is not a recent invention.

1946

"Adnotationes in opus 'Mater Coredemptrix' a Patre N. Garcia conscriptum," Father X. Garcia, notes the need for The Blessed Virgin's Coredemption., *Marianum* 8 (1946): 277–83.

1947

"Testimonia saeculi XVIII de Beata Virgine Co-redemptrice," Testimony of the Blessed Virgin's Coredemption in 18th Century writers., *Marianum* 9 (1947): 37–63.

"Romanorum Pontificum doctrina de Beata Virgine Co-redemptrice," The Papal doctrine of Mary's Coredemption., *Marianum* 9 (1947): 161–83.

1948

"De Corredemptione Beatae Virginis Mariae in quibusdam postulatis ad sanctam Sedem delatis," The coredemption of the Blessed Virgin Mary in some petitions submitted to the Holy See., *Miscellanea Francescana* 48 (1948): 85-90.

"The Definability of Mary's Assumption," *American Ecclesiastical Review* 118 (1948):161–77.

"Episcoporum doctrina de Beata Virgine Corredemptrice," Episcopal doctrine of the Blessed Virgin Mary., *Marianum* 10 (1948): 211–58.

Book Review:

Clement Dillenschneider, C.S.S.R., *Marie au service de notre redemption*, Mary in the service of our redemption., *Marianum* 10 (1948): 307–08.

1949

"Mary's Coredemption According to Nineteenth Century Italian Writers," *Marianum* 11 (1949): 407–22.

"Mary's Coredemption in the Teaching of Pope Pius XII," *American Ecclesiastical Review* 121 (1949): 353–61.

1950

De Corredemptione Beatae Virginis Mariae apud scriptores saeculi XVII, The coredemption of the Blessed Virgin in writers of the Seventeenth century., Pontificium Athenaeum Antonianum de Urbe. Facultas Theologica. *Dissertation ad lauream* No. 61 (Civitas Vaticana: Typis Polyglottis Vaticanis, 1950), v, 198–322.

De Corredemptione Beatae Virginis Mariae. Disquisitio positiva, Positive inquiry of the Coredemptive role of the Virgin Mary., Theology Series, No. 2 (Civitas Vaticana, Typis Polyglottis Vaticanis, 1950), 643 pp.

"The Mariological Movement in the World Today," *Marian Studies* 1 (1950): 25–45.

"The Problem of Our Lady's Coredemption," *American Ecclesiastical Review* 123 (1950): 32–51.

1951

"The Apostolic Constitution 'Munificentissimus Deus' and Our Blessed Lady's Coredemption," *American Ecclesiastical Review* 125 (1951): 255–73.

"The Apostolic Constitution 'Munificentissimus Deus' and Our Lady's Coredemption," *Marianum* 13 (1951): 237–56.

1952

"Mary's Co-redemption in the Teaching of Pope Pius XII," in J.C. Fenton and E.D. Bedard, *Studies in Praise of Our Blessed Mother: Selections from the American Ecclesiastical Review*, (Washington, D.C., Catholic University of America Press, 1952), 162–70.

"Our Lady's Coredemption in the Marian Literature of Nineteenth Century America," *Marianum* 14 (1952): 49–63.

"Mary, Mediatrix of all Graces," *Our Lady's Digest* 6 (March 1952): 417–26.

1953

"El Episcopado y el problema de la Corredencion (Carta abierta al Rdo P.N. Garcia)," The Episcopate and the problem of Coredemption., *Marianum* 15 (1953): 375–83.

1955

Mariology, ed. J. B. Carol, O.F.M. vol. 1 (Milwaukee, Bruce Pub Co., 1955), xvi, 1–434.

"Mary, Coredemptrix," in *In Praise of Mary*, ed. R.J. Treece (St. Meinrad, IN, 1955), 108–20.

1956

Fundamentals of Mariology (New York, Benziger, 1956), xx, 1–203. This is a book providing the primary content Carol would teach seminarians, religious and priests. It is referenced here because of his treatment of Mary as Coredemptrix of mankind. Carol says more important than the word Coredemptrix is the doctrine conveyed by the word. He looks at six points to address this.

1957

Mariology, ed. J. B. Carol O.F.M., vol. 2, (Milwaukee, Bruce Pub Co., 1957), xii, 1-606. This article looks at Mary's position in the economy of salvation (see, P. 377), and her cooperation with Jesus, in a mediately and immediately way (P. 379). He looks at the Ordinary Magisterium, the teaching of Tradition, nature and modalities of her Coredemption and looks at difficulties and solutions.

"Our Lady's Co-redemption," in *Mariology*, ed. J. B. Carol, (Milwaukee: Bruce Pub. Co., 1957), 2: 377–425.

1964

Mariologia, por una comision internatcional de especialistas bajo la presidencia de J. B. Carol. Traduccion de Maria Angeles G. Carega. Prologo sobre la mariologia en el Concilio Vaticano II, por Narciso GarciaGarces. (Madrid, Biblioteca de Autores Cristianos, 1964), xvii, 1–997 (= Biblioteca de Autores Cristianos, seccion II, Teologia y Canones, 242). Translation into Spanish of Mariology, vols. 1–2.

"Corredencion de Nuestra Senora," in *Mariologia*, (Madrid 1964), 760–804.

1967

"Mary, Blessed Virgin, II (in theology) [Mediatrix of All Graces]," in *New Catholic Encyclopedia* (15 vols.; New York: McGraw Hill, 1967), 9: 359–64.

1976

"Religious Congregation Honors Mary as Co-redemptrix," *Marianum* 38 (1976): 529–530.

"Dr. J. M. Alonso on Mary's Mediation," *Ephemerides Mariologicae* 26 (1976): 159–167.

1978

"Mary's Coredemption in a Petition of the Cuban Hierarchy to Pius XII," *Marianum* 40 (1978), pp. 440–44.

1.20. Note of Explanation Concerning Bibliography:

The *Primary Sources* covering a period from 1935-1986, deal with the works published by Father Juniper B. Carol applicable to the thesis. These are the main works, or as I call them *Primary Sources,* used from Carol in the formulation of this thesis. A more thorough list of his publication Coredemption, the *Debitum* and the Predestination of Mary can be found in Appendix D. The reasons for these primary texts utilized over and against the others in the appendix are twofold. First, the three Mariological areas of emphasis are addressed convincingly by the ones in this primary section and therefore do Carol's perspective justice. Second, the thesis would not have been enhanced by some of the lesser articles or book reviews since I have utilized his primary publications. Since I have provided an annotated bibliography at the beginning and end of each chapter addressing a Marian theme, I have simply provided the reader with the *Primary Sources* in a chronological order.

The *Secondary Sources* point the reader to articles, Marian publications and books complimenting Carols Marian focus as demonstrated in this thesis and are about Carol's Mariology or someone's reference to Carol and his work. I have placed these in alphabetical order. This is *Secondary* only because, while important, they were not published by Carol.

Finally, the phone interviews and email dialogue with those few who knew Carol were of great value in disclosing information about Father Carol as a man and Mariologist. I have provided their names and the dates of the interviews.

1.21. Primary Sources (Father Juniper B. Carol, O.F.M., publications).

Carol, Father Juniper B. O.F.M.

———. "Questionnaire for IV Year Theologians", Greenville, TN, Tusculum College, (1935).

———. "In Defense of the Title of Co-redemptrix" *Homiletic and Pastoral Review,* 36 (New York, NY, 1936), 1197-1199.

———. "The Holy See and the Title of 'Coredemptrix'," *Homiletic and Pastoral Review,* (New York, NY; J.F. Wagner, 1937), 746–748.

———. *Mariology*, ed. J. B. Carol, O.F.M., vol. 1., (Milwaukee, The Bruce Publishing Company, 1955). xvi,1-434.

———. "By Way of Introduction.", *Mariology,* ed. J. B. Carol, O.F.M., vol. 1., (Milwaukee, The Bruce Publishing Company, 1955). ix-xii.

———. *Fundamentals of Mariology*, (New York, NY, Benziger Brothers Inc.,1956), xx, 1-203.

———. *Mariology*, ed. J. B. Carol, O.F.M., vol. 2, "Our Lady's Coredemption.", (Milwaukee, The Bruce Publishing Company, 1957). Xii, 1-606.

———. "Kennedy for President? A Catholic Priest Says 'No'." *Human Events*, 17, No. 30. Section 111-B (July 28,1960), 313.

———. "Prefatory Note.", (Editor)., *Mariology* 3, (Milwaukee, The Bruce Publishing Company, 1961).

———. *A History of the Controversy Over the "Debitum Peccati."* Franciscan Institute Publications. Theology Series, No. 9, ed. George Marcil, O.F.M. (St. Bonaventure, NY, The Franciscan Institute of St. Bonaventure University, 1978), xiii, 1-260.

———. *The Absolute Primacy and Predestination of Jesus and His Virgin Mother*, (Chicago: Franciscan Herald Press, 1981), xiii, 1-177.

Pancheri, Francis Xavier, O.F.M.Conv., *The Universal Primacy of Christ*, translated and adapted from the Italian edition by

Juniper B. Carol, O.F.M. (Front Royal, VA: Christendom Publications, 1984), x,1-144.

———. *Why Jesus Christ?, Thomistic, Scotistic and Conciliatory Perspectives* (Manassas, VA, Trinity Communications, 1986), xviii, 1-531.

Letters of Correspondence between Carol and Koehler:[387]

———. Secretary of Mariological Society of America (June 24, 1976).

———. Personal letter to Father Koehler (June 4, 1979).

———. Letter between Koehler and Carol on (March 1, 1979).

———. Correspondence between Carol and Koehler, (May 14, 1979).

———. Correspondence between Carol and Koehler, (November 12, 1979).

———. Correspondence between Carol and Koehler, June 2, 1980.

———. Correspondence November 21, 1980.

———. Correspondence between Carol and Koehler, (July 18, 1988).

———. Correspondence between Carol and Koehler, (July 25, 1988).

———. Correspondence between Carol and Koehler, (August 1, 1988).

———. Correspondence between Carol and Koehler, (February 9, 1989).

———. Correspondence between Carol and Koehler, (December 8, 1982).

———. Correspondence between Carol and Rev. George F. Mclean, O.M.I. of Catholic University of America on (July 23, 1976).

Marian Studies:[388]

———. "The Mariological Movement in the World Today.",

---

[387] These letters covered a period from 1979-1982. There are a couple other letters that I have included. I have copies I made from the Marian Library's files on Carol.

[388] I have put these together and in order of their publication date.

Marian Studies 1 (Washington, D.C., The Mariological Society of America, Holy Name College, 1950).

_____. Report on the New York Convention, *Marian Studies* 3 (1952), 5–8. An overview of the convention by Carol.

_____. Report on the Cleveland Convention, *Marian Studies* 4 (1953), 5–9. An overview of the convention by Carol.

_____. Report on the Washington [D.C.] Convention, *Marian Studies* 5 (1954),5–12. An overview of the convention by Carol.

_____. "Our Lady's Immunity from the Debt of Sin.", *Marian Studies* 6 (1955). 166-167.

_____. "Report on the New York Convention," *Marian Studies* 7 (1956), 5–11. An overview of the convention by Carol.

_____. Report on the Chicago Convention, *Marian Studies* 8 (1957), 5–12. An overview of the convention by Carol.

_____. Report on the Dayton Convention, *Marian Studies* 9 (1958), 5–14. An overview of the convention by Carol.

_____. Report on the Paterson Convention, *Marian Studies* 10 (1959), 5–12. An overview of the convention by Carol.

_____. Report on the Detroit Convention, *Marian Studies* 11 (1960), 5–12. An overview of the convention by Carol.

_____. Report on the Pittsburgh Convention, *Marian Studies* 12 (1961), 15–20. An overview of the convention by Carol.

_____. Report on the New Orleans Convention, *Marian Studies* 13 (1962), 13–16. Report on convention for the MSA by Carol.

_____. Report on the Boston Convention, *Marian Studies* 14 (1963), 7-16. Report on convention for the MSA by Carol.

_____. Report on the Kansas City Convention, *Marian Studies* 15 (1964), 7–11. Report on convention for the MSA by Carol.

_____. Report on the Philadelphia Convention, *Marian Studies* 16 (1965), 7–10. Report on convention for the MSA by Carol.

_____. Report on the Louisville Convention, *Marian Studies* 17 (1966), 7–12. Report on convention for the MSA by Carol.

_____. Report on the North Palm Beach Convention, *Marian Studies* 18 (1967),7–11. Report on convention for the MSA by Carol.

_____. Report on the Dayton Convention, *Marian Studies* 19 (1968), 14–19. Report on convention for the MSA by Carol.

_____. Report on the Tampa Convention, *Marian Studies* 20 (1969), 14–21. Report on convention for the MSA by Carol.

_____. Report on the [St. Petersburgh Beach] Convention, *Marian Studies* 22 (1971), 7–12. Report on convention for the MSA by Carol.

_____. Report on the San Antonio Convention, *Marian Studies* 23 (1972), 7–11. Report on convention for the MSA by Carol.

_____. Report on the St. Louis Convention, *Marian Studies* 24 (1973), 5–11. Report on convention for the MSA by Carol.

_____. Presentation [for the Silver Jubilee of the Mariological Society of America], *Marian Studies* 25 (1974), 5–7.

_____. Report on the Atlanta Convention, *Marian Studies* 26 (1975), 5–8. Report on convention for the MSA by Carol.

_____. Report on the Washington, D.C. Convention, *Marian Studies* 27 (1976),5–10. Report on convention for the MSA by Carol.

_____. "The Blessed Virgin and the 'Debitum Peccati.' A Bibliographical Conspectus", *Marian Studies* 28 (1977)

_____. Report on the North Palm Beach Convention, *Marian Studies* 28 (1977), 5–9. Report on convention for the MSA by Carol.

_____. Report on the Baltimore, Md. Convention, *Marian Studies* 29 (1978), 5–11. Report on convention for the MSA by Carol.

———. "Reflections on the Problem of Mary's Preservative Redemption." *Marian Studies* 30 (The Mariological Society of America, 1979). 19-88.

_____. The Absolute Predestination of the Blessed Virgin Mary, *Marian Studies* 31 (1980), 172–238.

_____. Memorial Tribute to Cardinal John J. Wright (1979), *Marian Studies* 31 (1980), 36–39.

1.22. Secondary Sources:

Athens, Mary Christine, B.V.M., "Mary in the American Catholic Church", U.S. Catholic Historian, Col. 8. No. 4, Bicentennial Symposium: Historians and Bishops in Dialogue (Fall, 1989), 103-116.

"Another Friar Named to Marian Commission." (NY, *The Provincial Annals* 6, 1947-48), 301.

Beatti, Tina, "Mary, Eve and the Church", *Maria* 2 (2001) 5–20. This paper was originally given as the Marian Study Center Candlemas Lecture, at Ushaw College, Durham, on Monday 31 January 2000.

Budwey, Stephanie A., "Mary, Star of Hope: Marian Congregational Song as an Expression of Devotion to the Blessed Virgin Mary in the United States from 1854 to 2010. The Hymn, Spring 2012, Vol. 63. No. 2. 7-17.

Calkins, Arthur B., "Mary CoRedemptrix: The Beloved Associate of Christ", *Mariology A Guide for Priests, Deacons, Seminarians, and Consecrated Persons.* (Santa Barbara, CA, Seat of Wisdom Books A Division of Queenship Publishing 2007), 339–409.

Carroll, Eamon R. O. Carm., "Magnificat: Remembrance and Praise. The Mariological Society of America 1949-1999." 50th Anniversary of the Mariological Society of America, "Evolution in Mariology, 1949-1999." *Marian Studies*, 50 (1999).

Catechism of the Catholic Church, (NY, An Image Book, Doubleday,1995).

Davis, Brian, and Evans, G.R., ed., *Anselm of Canterbury The Major Works*, (NY, Oxford University Press 1998).

Domas, Anna Wirtz, *Mary USA*, (Huntington, IN: *Our Sunday Visitor, Inc.*, 1978).

Fehlner, Peter D. O.F.M.Conv., "Fr. Juniper B. Carol, O.F.M.: *His Mariology and Scholarly Achievement." Marian Studies* 43 (Dayton, OH, The Mariological Society of America, 1992).

Flannery, O.P., *Vatican Council II, Dei Verbum, Nostra Aetate, Lumen Gentium,* (NY, Costello Publishing Company, Inc., 1975).

"Fr. Carmel Lluria," (NY, *The Provincial Annals* 57, 2008).

Catholic News. "Fr. Carol Is Given Double Honor at Meeting of Mariologists Here". Jan. 19, 1952. November 23, 1949.

"Fr Juniper B. Carol," (NY, *The Provincial Annals* 40, 1991), 109–112.

"Fr. Juniper Carol Marks Silver Jubilee." (NY, *The Provincial Annals* 1960), 121.

Haynes, Grace, *The Daddy Haynes Story, The Life of Professor Landon Carter Haynes,* (Charlotte, NC, Morrison Printing CO., 1968).

Koehler, Theodore A., S.M. "In Homage to the Founder of the Mariological Society of America Juniper Benjamin Carol, O.F.M. (1911-1990)", *Ephemerides Mariologiae, Annus LIII- Fasc. II - n. 142-* (Rome, *1991).*

Kolbe, St. Maximilian M., *St. Maximilian M. Kolbe Martyr of Charity. Pneumatalogist, His Theology of the Holy Spirit* (Academy of The Immaculate, 2004), 1-199.

Kozack, Jessica Catherine, *The Primacy of Christ as the Foundation of the Coredemption: The Mariology of Fr. Juniper B. Carol, O.F.M. (1911-1990).* Master's Thesis from University of Dayton, (Aug. 2015).

Lumpkin, Ilene Greenfield, "Berkeley College Honors Missionary Sisters of the Immaculate Conception at 75th Anniversary Celebration." (Berkeley College, September 27, 2006; 2007).

Manelli, Rev. Stefano F.F.I. "Marian Coredemption in the Hagiography of the 20th Century." *Mary Coredemptrix Doctrinal Issues Today*, (Queenship Publishing, 2002), 191-262.

Manteau-Bonamy, H.M., O.P., *Immaculate Conception and the Holy Spirit: The Marian Teachings of Father Kolbe*, (NY, Prow Books/Franciscan Marytown Press, 1977).

Marianum, Annus LIII-Fasc. II-n. (Rome, 1991) 142. (book review).

McCurry, James O.F.M.Conv. "Fr. Juniper B. Carol, O.F.M., 1911-1990: *Vir Catholicus et Totus Apostolicus." Marian Studies* 42 (1991).

Miravalle, Mark, S.T.D., *Mary Coredemptrix, Mediatrix, Advocate*. (Santa Barbara, CA, Queenship Publishing, 1993).

Miravalle, Mark, S.T.D., *Mary Coredemptrix, Mediatrix, Advocate*. (Santa Barbara, CA, Queenship Publishing, 1993).

Olivares, Jose De, *Our Islands and Their People as seen with Camera and Pencil*, (St. Louis, New York, Chicago and Atlanta, Introduced   by Major-General Joseph Wheeler. N. D. Thompson Publishing Company, 1899).

"One Hundred and Thirtieth Year, *Tusculum College, Annual Catalogue, 1923-1924 With Announcements for 1924-1925*," Greenville, TN, Published by Tusculum College, (May 1924).

Pope Pius IX, *Ineffabilis Deus*, (Boston, MA, St. Paul Books and Media).

"Rev. Fr. Juniper Carol, O.F.M. Was Rewarded". (NY, *The Provincial Annals* 8, No. 3, 1950), 49–50.

The Siena News: Newspaper of America's Youngest College. "Cardinals Have Siena Friends," 7. No. 9., February 28, 1946.

———. "Faculty Members Aid in Jubilee Drive," 3. No. 4. October 18,1940.

———. "Forum Presents Spring Musical," 3. No. 5. May 2, 1947.

———. "Forum Rule Changes Hands," 9. No. 2., October 8, 1947.

———. "Fr. Juniper   Aids Bolivian Pilot After Fatal Crash," 9, No. 10.

———. "French Family Prayer Card Available," 24, No. 13. Dec. 14, 1962.

———. "Opera Forum Sponsors Grand Opera Concert," 7, No. 2. October 29, 1945.

———. "Skull-Cap of Pius XII Prided Possession of Fr. Juniper," 3. No. 5. October 25, 1940.

————. "Student Senate Enters New Field; Sponsors Concert,"
  10, No. 5. October 22, 1948.

The Catholic Answer Bible, *NAB*. (Wichita, KS, Fireside
  Catholic   Publishing, Our Sunday Visitor, Inc. DeVore and
  Sons, Inc., 2002).

Thompson, Thomas A., S.M., "Magnificat: Remembrance and
  Praise. The Mariological Society of America 1949-1999."
  50th Anniversary of the Mariological Society of America,
  "Evolution in Mariology, 1949-1999." *Marian Studies*, 50
  (1999).

Spaeth, Paul J., "History of the Franciscan Institute Library."
  (Bonaventure, NY, Bonaventure University, *Franciscan
  Studies* 51, 1991).

White, Joseph M., *Peace and God in America, A History of
  Holy Name Province Order of Friars Minor 1850s To The
  Present*. (New York, NY, Holy Name Province, 2004).

Websites:
www.yandex.com (aid in Latin translation)
www.newadvent.org (aid in defining theologians and their
  work)
www.wikipedia.com (aid in defining theologians and their
  work)
www.EWTN.com (aid in defining theologians and their work)
www.Franciscanmedia.org (aid in defining theologians and their
  work)
www.hnp.org (Holy Name Province)

1.23.   Phone Interviews (chronological):

Father Peter Fehlner 8/14/2012

Father Giles Bello, O.F.M. 12/5/2012

Father Larry Burk, O.F.M. 12/5/2012

Sister Sheila Madden with the Missionary Sisters of the
Immaculate Conception: 12/11/2012

Sister Jane Abeln 12/14/2012

Father Dominic Monti, O.F.M. 2/4/2013

Appendix A: Missionary Sisters of the Immaculate Conception Interviews

This thesis presents first person accounts from those who knew Father Carol in an academic capacity. These accounts offer the reader a picture of Carol as both an educator and a man. It was my intention to try and gain a deeper understanding of who Carol was beyond the realm of publications. The appendix has the interview of two Missionary Sisters of the Immaculate Conception, which gives a unique credibility to the subject of this thesis.

In each of these two interviews I asked many of the same questions and would try to find ways to build off what they initially recalled. Since their reflections were when they were young religious postulants who encountered Father Carol in an academic and priestly environment their reflections had some similarities. Some of the questions were based on his teaching style. Did he use the books he'd written for the courses he taught? Did he have a strong Cuban accent? Did he speak about his family at all? Was he serious or funny in the classroom? I wanted to get a feel for who he was as a person and not so much the content of his teachings.

Sister Sheila Madden: Phone interview with Chris Padgett on 12/11/2012.

The Sister Sheila Madden, the first Missionary Sisters of the Immaculate Conception that I interviewed had a few wonderful insights concerning Father Carol. Sister Madden came into the order in 1956, which was in Patterson, NJ, now called Woodland Park. She remembers that Father Carol lived at the convent which was their Motherhouse. The convent had a residence for women who were widowed, and Father Carol stayed in that area with them and obviously not with the sisters. Back then, around three hundred sisters were in their order, which became a province in 1960. Their order reached into California, Maine, Texas and other areas around the country. In 1958 Sister Sheila had just been professed. She was only there with Father Carol for a little bit, until leaving for Texas in 1960. Sister Madden remembers that Father Carol did the theology and mathematics courses for the religious. They had exposition every day and he would arrive in the early evenings for benediction. She knew that he did other things around the area. I was curious if he had a distinct Cuban accent, but she did not notice anything that implied he was not from the states. Sister Sheila had Father Juniper as a theology professor and did not even know he was from Cuba. For Sister, there wasn't even a hint of an accent, and not a mention of the early years in Cuba, nor could she recall a word concerning his family.[389]

Sister Madden said that Father Juniper was someone who had quite a flair for the dramatic. She said he should have been a Shakespearian actor. "He would come into the classes, in fact, one time he came dashing into the room, (eleven sisters were present) jumped right up on the table and started to give them the lecture." She said they were all shocked and could not pay attention to the details. "That's like a breath of fresh air coming in" she said. Sister Madden also said that Father Carol was a spiritual person. She had him for two courses; one theology and the other in Mariology. Sister felt Father Carol was always very interesting, dramatic, and brought good information to them.

---

[389] Interview with Sister Sheila Madden of the Missionary Sisters of the Immaculate Conception: 12/11/2012.

Sister remembered that Father Carol was a friend of Bishop Cardinal Wright, and that Father would bring in some of the Cardinal's writings and would discuss them with the sisters. I asked her if the Sisters knew of any little quirk or topic that would get him off tangent in the classroom, but she insisted that you could not get him off on a tangent, and you did not ask questions in the middle of his class. He gave his lecture and then he would ask the students questions to see if they understood the topic. Sister said that Father Carol usually left right after the lecture and that he always wore his habit. Sister Madden recalls that she was in Texas when he left, and they were notified when Father Carol passed away.

Originally the Missionary Sisters of the Immaculate Conception of the Mother of God were called the Franciscan Sisters of the Immaculate Conception. They would eventually drop the Franciscan portion for their official title. Sister remembers that Father Carol did use his books as primary texts, but the religious did not know that. I asked her if Father Carol was ever at a loss for words, and she laughed saying, "Oh, God no!" "Never!" She said that he never did anything with audio visual, and if there was anything with music it was him singing it.

Concerning his priestly duties, Sister Sheila relayed that Father Carol did not have other priests come up to concelebrate Mass but did not know if this was a personal choice. The Franciscan Monastery was in Patterson, and she currently resides at St. Bonaventure, where the monastery was. The classes were structured in 45-minute segments and they would meet every day during the week.

Sister also recalled, "Father Carol never had any tangents in which he spoke about the culture or politics within the classroom, although we know his feelings about Communism and Kennedy from earlier publications." She remembers that he never swore but did possibly go into Latin every so often. Father Juniper Carol stuck to what he wanted to get across to the students that particular day. Sister said that contact with them was not really "up close." He was always a distance from them when in class and would walk around a lot. She said that Father Carol did not talk about himself with the religious. I wondered if Father Carol had any pets that the sisters would have remembered, but she said that he did not.

Sister Jane Abeln, Missionary Sisters of the Immaculate Conception: Phone interview with Chris Padgett on 12/14/2012.

The second interview I conducted was with Sister Jane Abeln on 12/14/2012, who was a young postulant when she met Father Carol during the late 50's. Sister Jane had Father Carol as a religion teacher, as well as her regular confessor and priest. She remembers that Father Carol celebrated Mass, Benediction and heard confessions for all of the sisters on a regular basis and she recalls that, "he was somewhat of a gregarious fellow; sort of a comedian."

I asked Sister Jane to reflect upon what Father Juniper was like as a teacher. She said, "He would always be jumping around. He was short, and when he taught, he tried to make the material lively by joking a little bit. He would dramatically emphasize that which was *De fide* and what was not. This was of great importance to Carol, and he wanted the religious in his classrooms to understand what Marian teachings were, *De Fide* and what was more of a theological opinion." Sister Jane said that Father Carol would explain the doctrine in a dry sort of way, and upon reflection it wasn't really exciting material to her. Sister said that at that time it was almost like he was simply listing different doctrines, what it meant and what kind it was. She remembers him saying, "This you have to believe and this you don't."

I asked, "Did Father Carol use the books he published to lecture to them as students?"

Sister knew he wrote a book, and guessed he was using his book during lectures, but they never purchased texts for the religion classes. I really wanted Sister Jane to try and give me an image of what Father Carol was like in person and she stated, "He was a rolly polly kind of guy that enjoyed joking about things."

Sister Jane mentioned that she didn't recall Father Carol eating or drinking in classes, but she only knew him for a couple of years.

Sister Jane was there in New Jersey from 1959 to about 1962, and after this time, she was sent for study elsewhere in the United States. When discussing her time with the other religious sisters and her interactions with Father Carol, Sister Jane repeatedly mentioned that all of this was pre-Second Vatican Council, and life for the religious back then was very routine and programed, especially concerning the way their convent was run. This time period for most religious, before the Second Vatican Council, was silent about the individual person. She thought this was applicable because when thinking back on Father Carol the priest, the teacher and the man, there was not a lot of information about him that was revealed in the classrooms, because according to Sister, it just didn't happen that way back then. Self-disclosure and personal reflection were not considered appropriate for a religious; whereas, it did not seem to be a matter of pride to talk about oneself in years following the Council.

According to Sister Jane, up until the late fifties and early sixties the Missionary Sisters and other religious were encouraged to almost forget themselves because it was prideful to share the background of your life with others. Sister Jane was only a postulant while Father Carol lived in the Holy Family residence for elderly women. The first floor of this building was set apart for his apartment. I asked Sister if she had ever visited Father Carol there, since many of the religious would clean his room. I was interested if she remembered the home being messy or clean, really anything that might shed a little light on Father Juniper outside of his teaching and religious duties. Sister said that she visited him there once to talk about a personal matter, but otherwise never would have had reason to be in that area. She felt he had a neatly kept living room, but while the first floor contained a number of rooms, she had not seen any of them, since she was not on the cleaning crew. She did say he was a neat person, and really someone who did not have a mess around him.

I asked Sister if she remembered him ever speaking about Communism in class. She recalls him speaking negatively of Communism, and this according to Sister was during the 1958–60-time period, which was a period of extreme sensitivity towards Communism, with Kennedy wading through the Cuban crisis.

Trying to stir some more reflections about Carol in the classroom, I asked Sister if he discussed many other theologians. She said that during classes he would talk about other theologians and what they said about theological matters, but it was all very rote. This is the doctrine, this is which professor or theologian is for it, and this is one who does not think this doctrine is true.

Knowing that Carol was publishing the Mariological compendiums during this time I asked if he used his text in classes. Sister said that Carol's Mariology book was likely used, the one published shortly before she had him as a professor. She knew he was known as a famous theologian but was disappointed that the class content wasn't more exciting. She said:

> He was so lively and joking. He would integrate humor to lighten things up during the presentation, trying to emphasize things in a dramatic way. *De Fide* would be said with dramatic emphasis. His class presentations were not done with a lot of deviation from the rote expression of what each doctrine meant. While he quoted theologians in connection with Mariological development and the road to and process in which the Church and earlier theologians looked into it.

I gathered that for a young postulant, she imagined these religious classes and their topic to be rather bland.

I wondered if Father Carol ever gave the students handouts, and she said that everything was verbal. There was not a primary textbook for the sisters since it was lecture driven. She said, "not a lot of interesting insights, just the facts." I then asked her if Father Carol allowed questions in his lectures and she said that he did. Apparently, sometimes Father Carol reacted dramatically to the questions which helped lighten the mood for the sisters.

Upon further reflection Sister remembers Carol had his own space to eat in the Holy Family dining room, but that it would not be proper for the sisters to eat there with him. Things were different before Vatican II and the separation between the priest and religious was stricter in that time than today. What I found very interesting, was Sister's remembrance of Carol's Marian devotion. She said: "He didn't come across as having a relationship with Mary. It seems more personal today." Sister Jane did not sense Father Carol had a personal relationship with Mary when he was talking about her. But again, she emphasized that this was the way things were back then. The sisters had a phrase: "The secret of the king," which was an example of this type of quiet spirituality: "A religious sister wouldn't talk about her relationship with Jesus which was fostered in prayer. It would be out of place to talk about it." Sister Jane felt that when Father Juniper talked about Mary, it was more of a formality than a relationship. She felt it was probably there, but they did not talk about it back then. It was the time, and he was a man of the time.

These interviews offer a small brief on the life of Father Carol beyond what theological stances can be gleaned from his publications.

Appendix B: Phone interview with Father Peter Fehlner, F.I. on 8/14/2012.

This thesis presents first person accounts from those who knew Father Carol in a personal and priestly capacity. Father Peter Fehlner F.I., offers the reader a picture of Carol as both a Mariologist and a man. It was my intention to try and gain a deeper understanding of who Carol was beyond the scope of his publications. This appendix has interviews with Father Fehlner, which gives a unique credibility to the subject of this thesis.

In my phone conversation with the Friar of the Immaculata, the now late Father Fehlner, I asked him to give me a small personal reflection about Father Juniper Carol. Father Fehlner said, "Juniper was a wonderful person. He had his convictions. Carol was very conservative about his liturgy. He wasn't a traditionalist. He could be humorous at times." I asked him if he could detect a Cuban accent at all and if he knew of Carol's political opinions. He said, "For Carol, English wasn't his first language. His grandfather came from Ireland and went to Cuba. Juniper was anti-communist, even speaking out against John F. Kennedy."

I asked him to talk about the cigars Father Carol smoked and Father Fehlner said, "He was always smoking cigars, right up to the day he died. Stunk up the convention room." For those who didn't like his cigar, he may have quipped, "You should try one yourself, you might like one." Of course, he smoked Cuban cigars.

Father Fehlner came to know Father Carol towards the end of Juniper's life. He found Father Juniper welcoming, cracking a few jokes, and when moments came where he was going to contest a theological point, he was very persistent, saying, "Juniper Carol was very firm in his convictions." Father Fehlner said Carol wasn't much for speculation; rather, a systematic study of the sources specific to the topic at hand would be necessary for publication. For those writing for publication in *Marian Studies*, there were strict qualifications. Twenty pages was the limit, which apparently Father Fehlner found troubling since he went too much into questions of theory for Carol's taste. Father Juniper Carol said that methodology has to serve a purpose. Father Fehlner also relayed that Carol was always going to celebrate the mass the way he learned but didn't concelebrate as far as he remembered. Fehlner said, Juniper was Latin, and used his hands a bit when he spoke. He wasn't exaggerating in his writings because he was methodical. Carol was proficient with the many languages he had mastered, and Father Fehlner thought he had the best private Marian library of its time. While Father Fehlner never knew him in public circles, he said that Carol always seemed to be open and friendly to others."[390]

Carol had strong opinions concerning political movements and communism as a whole. Father Peter Fehlner, F. I., shared his understanding of Carol on this subject with me on August 14th, 2012. Fehlner emphasized Carol's anti-communist stance, mentioning even his opposition to the 1960 candidacy of John F. Kennedy, which was published in *The Wanderer*.[391] According to Fehlner, "In 1960 Carol gave a communion breakfast talk in Patterson, NJ, in which he described Kennedy (not yet nominated as Democratic candidate to succeed Eisenhower) as a left-wing liberal committed to

---

[390] Phone interview with Fr. Peter Fehlner. August 14, 2012.
[391] See "Fr. Juniper Carol," (*Provincial Annals* 40, 1991), 111., and from interview on Aug. 14, 2012.

continuing US support for Castro, for whom no good Catholic could in conscience support. The talk was reported by *The Wanderer* and came to the attention of Cardinal Spellman who then requested the Holy Name Provence silence him and transfer him as far away from New York as possible. He was sent to Florida, where he remained as I recall not merely 10 years, but almost to the late 80's." For many readers, this assessment of Kennedy did not go over well. In an email on February 5, 2013 Father Fehlner stated:

> Fr. Juniper once remarked to me in the course of a conversation about matters scotistic that it was difficult for him to submit anything favorable to Scotus for publication in The Wanderer, because the weekly was so exclusively thomist and treated everything favorable to Scotus as leading to modernism, even if coming for so staunch a defender of tradition. I think there was and still are objective grounds for agreeing with Fr. Juniper's estimate. But I also think his association with The Wanderer may also have been objected to by the more liberal orientated friars of Holy Name Province for reasons independent of Scotistic-Thomistic polemics.[392]

Father Fehlner states that Father Carol never went back to Cuba after leaving and was certain Kennedy was not going to save or solve the problems in which Cuba now found itself entrenched.[393]

---

[392] Fr. Fehlner's email to Chris Padgett on Feb. 5, 2013.
[393] Phone interview with Fr. Peter Fehlner, August 14, 2012.

Carol's opinion on Kennedy is also found in his 1960 article, "Kennedy for President? A Catholic Priest Says 'No'." *Human Events*. After defining liberalism as, "a congeries of pernicious fallacies, a strange combination of muddled thinking and ill-defined, misty attitudes on such heterogeneous subjects as economics, sociology, politics, philosophy and even religion,"[394] Carol states, "The election of Kennedy would bring about, more government interference and control; more spending on welfare measures; the eventual admission of Red China to the United Nations; the gradual surrender of our constitutional sovereignty to a World Court made up mostly of our enemies; the probable appointment of visionary Adlai Stevenson as Secretary of State, with its consequent crawling appeasement of the Reds; and, of course, the packing of the Supreme Court with "liberal" ideologues who will make shambles of our security laws. But why go on? The foregoing should be enough to chill the enthusiasm of the most fanatic Kennedy backer."[395]

---

[394] Rev. Juniper B. Carol, O.F.M., "Kennedy for President? A Catholic Priest Says 'No'." *Human Events*, 17, No. 30.-Section 111-B (July 28,1960), 313–314.

[395] Rev. Juniper B. Carol, O.F.M., "Kennedy for President? A Catholic Priest Says 'No'." *Human Events*, 17, No. 30.-Section 111-B (July 28,1960), 313–314.

Appendix C: Personal Reflection on Father Carol by Father Giles Bello, O.F.M., Father Larry Burke, O.F.M., and Father Dominic Monti, O.F.M.

In an attempt to get more first-hand material from Franciscan friars who would have remembered Father Carol, there were a number of difficulties. It seemed most of the Holy Name Province friars who would have remembered Father Carol had already passed away. There were only a few friars at the Franciscan infirmary who knew Father Carol, the first was Father Giles Bello, O.F.M., whose classmate was Carmel Lluria, O.F.M. (Carol's nephew), followed by Father Larry Burke, O.F.M. who is 92 years old, and Father Dominic Monti who only met Carol a couple of times but was able to provide important information. I spoke with Father Burke and Bello on December 5th, 2012 and entered into an email correspondence with Father Monti the end of 2012 and into the beginning of 2013. We spoke February 4th, 2013 to clarify a number of things. Father Monti is the only Friar I spoke with who is still alive in 2019.

Father Giles Bello, O.F.M.

When I asked Father Giles if he remembered Father Juniper, he said yes, because of his classmate Carmel Lluria. When I asked him if he met Father Carol, Bello said: "I can't hear you." So, yelling into the phone I asked again, "Did you ever meet Father Carol?" to which Bello responded, "I still can't hear you." While this is humorous, the difficulty of gathering first-hand accounts on Father Carol was evident in my research endeavors. Father Bello, less than nine months away, passed away September 2, 2013.[396]

Father Larry Burke, O.F.M.

Father Larry Burke was lucid and articulate, and apparently his phone worked accordingly. He had a wonderful story he remembered about Father Carol. Father Larry said "Father Carol came around one day and had a car for his personal use. Driving up, Carol asked if I wanted to take a ride with him. I can't remember if he or Juniper was the one driving, but as we went to the city of Paterson, into that area on the side where the religious Sisters were, riding in the car we came upon the scene of an accident. I ask if they should stop and Juniper said yes, that he would talk to the people involved in the accident. There was someone who was hurt, and they were Spanish speaking people." Father Burke thought how providential it was that they just happened to be driving by during their time of need and Father Carol, fluent in Spanish, was able to be a great comfort to them as a priest in their moment of need.

Another interesting account that shows the role language played in such occasions of ministry is recounted by the Siena college student newspaper when Father Juniper visited a depressed pilot.

> The Rev. Juniper Carol OFM, formerly professor
> of Spanish at Siena College, recently was
> instrumental in aiding Eric Rios Bridoux,
> Bolivian pilot whose plane collided with an

---

[396] See, Franciscan Friars, Holy Name Province website, https://hnp.org/who-we-are/our-friars/deceased-friars/giles-bello/

airliner over Washington and caused the death of 55 persons... He was suffering from a broken back, several broken ribs, pneumonia and multiple cuts, and seemed unconcerned whether he lived or died. Fr. Juniper, a native of Cuba, was asked to visit the pilot because of his fluent knowledge of Spanish, which Bridoux speaks. He administered Extreme Unction and heard Bridoux's confession. According to Fr. Juniper, "the pilot seemed in much better spirits when I left him after talking with him for a short time, consoling him, and promising to visit him again."[397]

The morning after the friar's visit, physicians described Bridoux's condition as 'generally improved.'[398]

When I asked Father Burke to share a little more about Carol he said: "Juniper Carol had a good sense of humor and spoke English well." He didn't detect any accent. "Carol laughed a lot. Seemed to get a kick out of life." Father Burke said that Juniper was, "Rather short, a little on the heavy side. A great laugh!" He said what I think many have felt, which is that Father Carol, "was the kind of guy that if he had an opinion it wouldn't be easy to change it." I was interested if the two priests interacted a lot socially and if he always wore his clerics. Father Burke reflected that Juniper Carol mostly was seen in his collar, but sometimes in his habit.

[397] "Fr. Juniper Aids Bolivian Pilot After Fatal Crash," *The Siena News: Newspaper of America's Youngest College*, 9, No. 10. November 23, 1949., 4.

[398] See "Fr. Juniper Aids Bolivian Pilot After Fatal Crash," *The Siena News: Newspaper of America's Youngest College*, 9, No. 10. November 23, 1949., 4.

Since I had asked Fehlner to speak a bit about Kennedy and Carol's opinion of Communism, I also asked Father Burke. Father Larry Burk, O.F.M. would reaffirm Fehlner's comments concerning Carol's lack of affection for Kennedy in an interview I had with him on December 5th, 2012. Burke said, "Carol didn't have much time for Castro, who wasn't helping the Cuban people much." For Carol, neither communism nor any fickle Catholic leader in politics would suffice. Concerning Kennedy's liberalism, according to Carol, he states:

> He (Kennedy) adopts an unrealistic approach to the gravest issue confronting us today, namely the Communist menace. Thus, he champions tolerance of subversives. He congratulates the Supreme Court when it rules in favor of Communists. He decries congressional committees and the F.B.I. when they try to expose the enemies of our country. He demands more hand-outs to so-called "neutralist" countries and even to Communist governments.[399]

Father Burke was the second Franciscan to speak about Carol in that way. Father Burke, 92 years of age, passed away September 18th, 2013.[400]

Father Dominic Monti, O.F.M.

Another personal reflection comes from Father Dominic Monti, O.F.M. He was referred to me by a friend, Father Rick

---

[399] Rev. Juniper B. Carol, O.F.M., "Kennedy for President? A Catholic Priest Says 'No'." Human Events, 17, No. 30.-Section 111-B (July 28,1960), 313.

[400] See, https://hnp.org/who-we-are/our-friars/deceased-friars/lawrence-burke/

Martignetti, O.F.M., who said that Father Monti is somewhat of an expert in the history of Franciscans. In my initial email with Father Dominic he mentioned that he met Father Carol a couple of times. Father Dominic said:

> I have to say that I did not know Fr Juniper that well myself—and I have been in the Province now since 1964 (professed in 1965, ordained in 1971). I did meet him several times, especially during my first years of teaching in Washington, when he came to look at the Mariological collection housed at our old house of studies, Holy Name College. This would have been in the period 1979-84.
>
> For the second half of his life—the part I would have known—he was really on the fringes of our Province. I certainly believe he was out of sympathy with theological trends and directions in the Province following Vatican II and was somewhat isolated in ministries of his own choosing. If you see from his biography, he served in various chaplaincies and other such 'one-man' assignments after 1967, living on his own—he moved into our friary in St Petersburg only in 1979. I know many older friars considered him somewhat of a prima donna, and one who did not 'pitch in' with the ministries other friars were engaged in. To them he seemed to take pride in a certain aristocratic (?) background that set him apart from the hoi polloi. In other words, he was never a 'community man.' Now, one must also say that the province during the 40s, 50s, 60s and 70s

was dominated by an Irish and Italian crowd from the Northeast (New England, New York, New Jersey, Pennsylvania), the sons of largely first and second generation immigrants, so there may have been a certain amount of prejudice on their part against this Latino. But my definite impression from them is that Juniper considered himself 'special,' a trait they disliked. I should also mention that Juniper's nephew from Cuba, Carmel Lluria, joined the province in 1949. He had a complete mental breakdown shortly after his first Mass in 1955 and was in and out of mental hospitals until his death in 2007. I think Juniper was somewhat self-conscious of this 'black sheep' in his family.'[401]

Father Dominic Monti, O.F.M. also mentioned that certain trends within the Holy Name Province could have easily been perceived by many, possibly even Carol, as liberal

Father Juniper's love for his friars and Franciscan order was known by those who were his peers, even if there were occasions to differ over theological applications and practices.

The world was in need of Our Lady more than ever.

It is interesting to note that of the various interviews I have had with people who knew Father Carol, not one person remembers Carol ever speaking about his siblings, or even his early years in Cuba.

---

[401] Email with Father Dominic Monti on 1/30/13.

203

Appendix D: Complete Bibliography and Publications of and about Rev. Juniper Benjamin Carol. O.F.M.[402]

---

[402] Gambero, Luigi, S.M., *Marianum* Ephemerides Mariologiae Annus LIII-Fasc.II-
n. 142-1991. This bibliography includes Koehler, Theodore, S.M.'s article, "In
Homage to the Founder of the Mariological Society of America Juniper Benjamin
Carol, O.F.M. (1911-1990)." 714–22. I will be supplementing Gambero's
Bibliography on Carol with the one from Father Peter D. Fehlner, O.F.M.Conv.,
"Fr. Juniper B. Carol, O.F.M.: *His Mariology and Scholarly Achievement.*"
Marian Studies 43 (1992): 17–59.

This bibliography is more thorough than the one at the end of my thesis. This includes publications from, on or about Carol. Since my thesis focused on three areas of Carol's publications it necessarily excluded a few listed below. I have combined the previously published bibliographies of Father Theodore Koehler, S.M., which is found at the end of his article, "In Homage to the Founder of the Mariological Society of America Juniper Benjamin Carol, O.F.M. (1911-1990)." 714–22., Father Gambero's along with Father Peter D. Fehlner, O.F.M.Conv., who included his at the end of his article, "Fr. Juniper B. Carol, O.F.M.: *His Mariology and Scholarly Achievement." Marian Studies* 43 (1992): 17–59. I have also included material published about Father Carol from *Siena News and The Provincial Annals*, which have annotations about the articles to lend the reader an understanding of what was within.

1936

"In Defense of the Title of Coredemprix," *Homiletic and Pastoral Review* 36 (1936): 1197–99.

1937

"The Theological Concept of Mediation and Co-redemption," *Ephemerides Theologicae Lovanienses* 14 (1937): 642–650.

"The Blessed Virgin's Co-redemption Vindicated. Short Observations on a Recent Work." (Quaracchi [Florence] 1937), pp. 30.

"The Holy See and the Title of 'Co-redemptrix'," *Homiletic and Pastoral Review* 37 (1937): 746–48.

1939

"De fundamento proximo Co-redemptionis Marianae," *Marianum* 1 (1939):173–187.

"Utrum Beatae Virginis Coredemptio sit in S. Scriptura formaliter revelata," *Marianum* 1 (1939): 283–326.

"Pio XII e la corredenzione di Maria," *Marianum* 1 (1939): 361–364.

"The Nature of the Blessed Virgin's Ontological Mediation," *Miscellanea Francescana* 39 (1939): 449–470.

"Episcopatus catholicus et Beatae Virginis Co-redemptio," *Ephemerides Theologicae Lovanienses* 10 (1939): 801–828.

Hermann Seiler., S.J., *Corredemptrix*, in *Marianum* 1 (1939): 237–40. (Book Review)

Hermann Seiler, S.J., *Corredemptrix*, in *Antonianum* 14 (1939): 412. (Book Review)

1940

"Pater H. Lennerz et problema de Co-redemptione Mariana," *Marianum* 2 (1940): 194–200.

"De Sanctorum Patrum Doctrina circa Beatae Virginis Corredemptionem," *Marianum* 2 (1940), pp. 256–66.

"Method in Mariology: An open letter to the Very Rev. Dr. Smith Concerning Mary's Co-redemption," *Clergy Review* 18 (1940): 371–75.

Paul Strater, S.J., *Die Seele der Gottesmutter; Father Canice, O.F.M. Cap., Mary: A Study of the Mother of God*; Luis Colomer, O.F.M., *La Virgen Maria*; Serapio De Iragui, O.F.M. Cap., *La mediacion de la Virgen en la himnografia latina del la Edad Media*, in Marianum 2 (1940): 203–205. (Book Review)

"Faculty Members Aid in Jubilee Drive," *Siena News*, Oct. 18, 1940. Vol. 3. No. 4. Loudonville, N.Y. Pg. 4. Published article from Siena college about Carol's participation in the Jubilee drive.

"Skull-Cap of Pius XII Prided Possession of Fr. Juniper," *Siena News*, Oct. 25, 1940. Vol. 3. No. 5. Loudonville, N.Y. Pg. 1. Published article from Siena college on Carol's reception of the Pope's skull cap

1941

"Doctrina de Beatae Virginis Coredemptione ab ortu usque ad prolapsum, aetatis Scholasticorum," *Miscellanea Francescana* 41 (1941): 248–66.

"Owls Give Another Birthday Party" *Siena News*, March 21, 1941. Vol. III. No. 20. Loudonville, N.Y. Pg. 1. Published article from Siena college about surprise birthday celebration for Father Sixtus O'Connor, which Carol attended.

1943

"Our Lady's Part in the Redemption According to Seventeenth-century writers," *Franciscan Studies* 24 (1943): 3–20; 143–58.

"Father Juniper Makes Reply to Protestant Attack on Pope," *Siena News*, February 19, 1943. Vol. V. No. 20. Loudonville, N.Y. Pg. 1, 4. Published article from Siena college about Carol's response to a Protestant's attack made against the Pope.

1945

"Opera Forum Sponsors Grand Opera Concert," *Siena News*, October 29, 1945. Vol. VII. No. 2. Loudonville, N.Y. Pg. 3. Four professional artists brought from New York City to Gibbons Hall at Siena College in large part due to Carol's work.

1946

"Adnotationes in opus 'Mater Corredemptrix' a Patre N. Garcia conscriptum," *Marianum* 8 (1946): 277–83.

"Forum to Hear Talk on Television," *Siena News*, February 15, 1946. Vol. VII. No. 8. Loudonville, N.Y. Pg. 1. The Opera Forum will hear a lecture on Opera and television by Mr. Robert B. Stone.

"Cardinals Have Siena Friends," *Siena News*, February 28, 1946. Vol. VII. No. 9. Loudonville, N.Y. Pg. 1. School news reports new Cardinals to the Church, with one of the 32 being Eminence, Manuel Arteaga y Betancourt, Archbishop of Havana, who was the godfather of Father Carol.

"Operatic Recital Coming April 25," *Siena News*, March 15, 1946. Vol. VII. Loudonville, N.Y. Pg. 1. Siena college news reports coming of Miss Barbara Troxwell, a distinguished American soprano.

"Peruvian Bishop Visits Campus on Return Visit from Rome," *Siena News*, October 16, 1946. Vol. VII. Loudonville, N.Y. Pg.

2. The school news reports visit of Carol's friend Most Reverend Bonaventure De Uriate, O.F.M. Bishop of Ucayali, Peru. They met in Spain in 1937.

1947

"Testimonia saeculi XVIII de Beata Virgine Co-redemptrice," *Marianum* 9 (1947): 37–63.

Romanorum Pontificum doctrina de Beata Virgine Co-redemptrice," *Marianum* 9 (1947): "161–83.

"Forum Decides on Membership Drive," *Siena News*, March 14, 1947. Vol. VIII. No. 8. Loudonville, N.Y. Pg. 1. Carol presided over the meeting to increase membership in the Forum.

"Forum Presents Spring Musical," *Siena News*, May. 2, 1947. Loudonville, N.Y. Pg. 4. Carol heads the Siena Opera Forum in 1947 and the school reports on the operatic musicale where soloists Ignatius Dinovo, Jean Raimundo and others performed.

"Dinner-Musicale Ends Forum Season," *Siena News*, May 29, 1947. Loudonville, N.Y. Pg. 3–4. A year end music forum with dinner and notable performers will end their season.

"Transfer Six Profs; Enroll Replacements," *Siena News*, September 22, 1947. Vol. IX. No. 1. Loudonville, N.Y. Pg. 1. The news reports Carol is one of six professors who are not on campus in 1947.

"Forum Rule Changes Hands," *Siena News*, Oct. 8, 1947. Vol. IX. No. 2. Loudonville, N.Y. Pg. 4. Carol is the founder of the Opera Forum and is the guest of honor at the farewell party Sept 21, 1947.

Another Friar Named to Marian Commission. The Provincial Annals Vol. 6 1947-48. Pg. 301. Father Carol made secretary general for the United States of the International Franciscan Commission of Mariology headquartered in Rome. See also *Siena News* May 21,1948.

1948

"De Corredemptione Beatae Virginis Mariae in quibusdam postulatis ad sanctam Sedem delatis," *Miscellanea Francescana* 48 (1948): 85-90.

"The Definibility of Mary's Assumption," *American Ecclesiastical Review* 118 (1948):161–77.

"Episcoporum doctrina de Beata Virgine Corredemptrice," *Marianum* 10 (1948): 211–58.

Clement Dillenschneider, C.S.S.R., *Marie au service de notre redemption*, in *Marianum* 10 (1948): 307–08. (Book Review).

Father Juniper Defends Thesis," *Siena News*, May 21, 1948. Vol. IX. Loudonville, N.Y. Pg. 1. Siena reports on Carol's defense.

"Fr. Juniper Home from Continental Trip—Gone Again," *Siena News*, September 20, 1948. Vol. X. No. 1. Loudonville, N.Y. Pg. 4. The paper reports on Carol, their former Spanish professor and founder of the Siena Opera Forum, who returned from a year in Europe only to leave to Holy Name College in Washington D.C. to complete a book on Mariology.

"Student Senate Enters New Field; Sponsors Concert," *Siena News*, Oct. 22, 1948. Vol. X. No. 5. Loudonville, N.Y. Pg. 1. Carol is mentioned as the one who started the Opera Forum.

Bradt, Cliff, "Fr. Juniper Home from Rome—and Glad," The Knickerbocker News, Albany, NY, Aug. 26, 1948, P. 2-13. Carol is reported back from Rome, where, according to Bradt, Father Carol was working on research for the new church encyclopedia.

1949

"Verso la definizione dogmatica dell'Assunta," *Marianum* 11 (1949): 88–94.

"Recent Literature on Mary's Assumption," *American Ecclesiastical Review* 120 (1949), pp. 376-387.

"Mary's Coredemption According to Nineteenth Century Italian Writers," *Marianum* 11 (1949): 407–22.

"Mary's Coredemption in the Teaching of Pope Pius XII," *American Ecclesiastical Review* 121 (1949): 353–61.

"Father Juniper Aids Bolivian Pilot After Fatal Crash," *Siena News*, November 23, 1949. Vol. XI. No. 10. Loudonville, N.Y. Pg. 4. Carol asked permission to visit a pilot whose plane crashed into an airliner over Washington killing 55 people. He administered Extreme Unction and heard the pilot, Eric Rios Bridoux's confession.

1950

De Corredemptione Beatae Virginis Mariae apud scriptores saeculi XVII, Pontificium Athenaeum Antonianum de Urbe. Facultas Theologica. *Dissertation ad lauream* No. 61 (Civitas Vaticana: Typis Polyglottis Vaticanis, 1950), v, 198–322.

De Corredemptione Beatae Virginis Mariae. Disquisitio positiva, Theology Series, No. 2 (Civitas Vaticana, Typis Polyglottis Vaticanis, 1950), 643 pp.

"The Mariological Movement in the World Today," *Marian Studies* 1 (1950): 25–45.

"The Problem of Our Lady's Coredemption," *American Ecclesiastical Review* 123 (1950): 32–51.

"The Recent Marian Congress at Pay-en-Velay," *American Ecclesiastical Review* 123 (1950): 273–83.

"Catholic Leaders Pay Tribute to 100-Year-Old Marianist Order," *Journal Herald*, May 17, 1950. (Carol is mentioned by the Journal Herald).

"Rev. Fr. Juniper Carol, O.F.M. Was Rewarded." *The Provincial Annals*. Vol. 8. 1950 n 3, 49–50. Carol was given the Marianist Award, and annual award, by the University of Dayton for outstanding service to Mary in America.

1951

"The Apostolic Constitution 'Munificentissimus Deus' and Our Blessed Lady's Coredemption," *American Ecclesiastical Review* 125 (1951): 255–73.

"The Apostolic Constitution 'Munificentissimus Deus' and Our Lady's Coredemption," *Marianum* 13 (1951): 237–56.

"A Bibliography of the Assumption," *Thomist* 14 (1951): 133–60. A bibliography of the Assumption is provided.

Dominic J. Unger, O.F.M. Cap., *Cardinal Newman and Apocalypse XII,* in *Marianum* 13 (1951): 198. (Book Review).

Eligius M. Buytaert, O.F.M., *The Immaculate Conception in the Writings of Ockham*, in *Marianum* 13 (1951): 200–201. (Book Review).

1952

"Mary's Co-redemption in the Teaching of Pope Pius XII," in J.C. Fenton and E.D. Bedard, *Studies in Praise of Our Blessed Mother: Selections from the American Ecclesiastical Review*, (Washington, D.C., Catholic University of America Press, 1952), 162–70.

"Report on the New York Convention," *Marian Studies* 3 (1952): 5–8. An overview of the convention by Carol.

"Our Lady's Coredemption in the Marian Literature of Nineteenth Century America," *Marianum* 14 (1952): 49–63.

"Mary, Mediatrix of all Graces," *Our Lady's Digest* 6 (March 1952): 417–26.

"Fr. Laurence Attends Mariology Convention," *Siena News*, January 14, 1952. Vol. XIII. No. 13. Loudonville, N.Y. Pg. 3. Father Carol mentioned as the Society's president.

"Fr. Carol is Given Double Honor at Meeting of Mariologists Here." *Catholic News*, Jan. 19, 1952. Carol is reelected at society president (the American Mariological Society) and $100. The reward was for, "the best contribution on Mariology made by any theologian in the past year."

1953

"Report on the Cleveland Convention," *Marian Studies* 4 (1953): 5–9. An overview of the convention by Carol.

"El Episcopado y el problema de la Corredencion (Carta abierta al Rdo P.N. Garcia)," *Marianum* 15 (1953): 375–83.

"Mary's Universal Queenship," *Our Lady's Digest* 8 (May 1953): 5-10.

1954

The Immaculate Conception and Mary's Death, Marian Reprint 27 (Dayton, Ohio, Marian Library, 1954): 8.

"Report on the Washington [D.C.] Convention," *Marian Studies* 5 (1954): 5–12. An overview of the convention by Carol.

"The Definition of the Immaculate Conception: Reflections on a Centenary," Our Lady's Digest 9 (Aug.-Sept. 1954): 108–111.

"On Mary's Virginity *in partu*: Rev. Dr. Carol on Dr. Henry's Article: "The Virgin Birth," *Homiletic and Pastoral Review* 54 (1954): 446-447.

1955

"Dangerous Marian Year Reefs," *Homiletic and Pastoral Review* 55 (May 1955), pp. 698–99.

Mariology, ed. J. B. Carol, O.F.M. vol. 1 (Milwaukee, Bruce Pub Co., 1955), xvi, 1–434.

"Mary, Coredemptrix," in *In Praise of Mary*, ed. R.J. Treece (St. Meinrad, IN, 1955), 108–20.

"Report on the St. Louis Convention," *Marian Studies* 6 (1955), 5–10. (An overview of the convention by Carol.).

"Our Lady's Immunity from the Debt of Sin," *Marian Studies* 6 (1955): 164–168.

"On 'Dangerous Marian Year Reefs'," *Homiletic and Pastoral Review* 55 (1955): 698-699.

1956

Fundamentals of Mariology (New York, Benziger, 1956), xx, 1–203. This is a book providing the primary fundamentals of Mariology Carol taught which would teach seminarians, religious and priests. It has been used to enhance this thesis in light of its treatment of Mary as Coredemptrix of mankind, the *debitum* and the predestination of Mary.

"Report on the New York Convention," *Marian Studies* 7 (1956): 5–11. An overview of the convention by Carol.

"Mary, the Mother of God, "*Our Lady's Digest* 11 (Dec. 1956): 207–11.

1957

Mariology, ed. J. B. Carol O.F.M., vol. 2, (Milwaukee, Bruce Pub Co., 1957), xii, 1-606.

"Our Lady's Co-redemption," in *Mariology*, ed. J. B. Carol, (Milwaukee: Bruce Pub. Co., 1957), 2: 377–425.

"Mary's Death," in *Queen of the Universe*, ed. Stanley G. Mathews (Saint Meinrad, Indiana, 1957), 44–54.

"Report on the Chicago Convention," *Marian Studies* 8 (1957): 5–12. An overview of the convention by Carol.

Catholic Teaching on Mary Explained to Non-Catholics," *Our Lady's Digest* 11 (March 1957): 326–30.

1958

"Report on the Dayton Convention," *Marian Studies* 9 (1958): 5–14. An overview of the convention by Carol.

"Maria y la Iglesia. Resena de una importante publicacion," *Marianum* 20 (1958): 95–104.

"Spiritual Lessons of Lourdes," *Our Lady's Digest* 13 (May 1958): 5–9.

1959

"Report on the Paterson Convention," *Marian Studies* 10 (1959): 5–12. An overview of the convention by Carol.

"Ex-Siena Teachers Assigned; Physics Instructor Named," *Siena News*, July 15, 1949. Carol is assigned to St. Bonaventure college.

Paterson Franciscan gets Theology Prize, *The Advocate*, June 26, 1959. This article talks of Carol being the recipient of the Cardinal Spellman Award for "outstanding achievement in theology" in 1959.

"Theology Professor is Award Recipient." *The Olean News,* July 2, 1959. Another article on the Spellman Award for Carol.

1960

"Report on the Detroit Convention," *Marian Studies* 11 (1960): 5–12. An overview of the convention by Carol.

"Fr. Juniper Carol Marks Silver Jubilee." *The Provincial Annals*. 1960. Pg. 121. Report on 25 years of Carol's ordination on Feb. 20, 1960.

1961

Mariology, ed. J. B. Carol O.F.M., vol. 3 (Milwaukee, Bruce Pub Co., 1961), xiv, 1-456.

"Immaculate Conception" in *American People's Encyclopedia* (20 vols.; Chicago: Spenser Press, 1961), 10: 954.

"Report on the Pittsburgh Convention," *Marian Studies* 12 (1961): 15–20. An overview of the convention by Carol.

1962

"Report on the New Orleans Convention," *Marian Studies* 13 (1962): 13–16. Report on convention for the MSA by Carol.

1963

"Report on the Boston Convention," *Marian Studies* 14 (1963): 7-16. Report on convention for the MSA by Carol.

"French Family Prayer Card Available," *Siena News*, December 14, 1962. Loudonville, N.Y. Pg. 4. Carol translated the prayer card into Spanish.

1964

Mariologia, por una comision internatcional de especialistas bajo la presidencia de J. B. Carol. Traduccion de Maria Angeles G. Carega. Prologo sobre la mariologia en el Concilio Vaticano II, por Narciso GarciaGarces. (Madrid, Biblioteca de Autores Cristianos, 1964), xvii, 1–997 (= Biblioteca de Autores

Cristianos, seccion II, Teologia y Canones, 242). Translation into Spanish of Mariology, vols. 1–2.

"Corredencion de Nuestras Senora," in *Mariologia*, (Madrid 1964), 760–804.

Report on the Kansas City Convention, *Marian Studies* 15 (1964), 7–11. Report on convention for the MSA by Carol.

"The History Behind May: Mary's Month," *Our Lady's Digest* 19 (1964): 22–5. An overview of the month of May.

1965

"Immaculate Conception," in *Encyclopedia Britannica* (24 vols.; Chicago, 1965), 11: 1101. Encyclopedic write up on the Immaculate Conception.

"Report on the Philadelphia Convention," *Marian Studies* 16 (1965): 7–10. Report on convention for the MSA by Carol.

1966

"Report on the Louisville Convention," *Marian Studies* 17 (1966): 7–12. Report on convention for the MSA by Carol.

1967

"Mariological Societies," in *New Catholic Encyclopedia*, (15 vols.; New York: McGraw Hill, 1967), 9: 223.

"Immaculate Conception, Missionary Sisters of (SMIC)," in *New Catholic Encyclopedia* (15 vols.; New York: McGraw hill, 1967), 7: 382.

"Mary, Blessed Virgin, II (in theology) [Mediatrix of All Graces]," in *New Catholic Encyclopedia* (15 vols.; New York: McGraw Hill, 1967), 9: 359–64.

"Report on the North Palm Beach Convention," *Marian Studies* 18 (1967): 7–11. Report on convention for the MSA by Carol.

1968

"Report on the Dayton Convention," *Marian Studies* 19 (1968): 14–19. Report on convention for the MSA by Carol.

1969

"Report on the Tampa Convention," *Marian Studies* 20 (1969): 14–21. Report on convention for the MSA by Carol.

1971

"Report on the [St. Petersburgh Beach] Convention," *Marian Studies* 22 (1971): 7–12. Report on convention for the MSA by Carol.

1972

"Report on the San Antonio Convention," *Marian Studies* 23 (1972): 7–11. Report on convention for the MSA by Carol.

1973

"Report on the St. Louis Convention," *Marian Studies* 24 (1973): 5–11. Report on convention for the MSA by Carol.

1974

"Presentation" [for the Silver Jubilee of the Mariological Society of America and Report on the St. Petersburg Beach Convention], *Marian Studies* 25 (1974): 5–7.

1975

"Report on the Atlanta Convention," *Marian Studies* 26 (1975): 5–8. Report on convention for the MSA by Carol.

1976

"Report on the Washington, D.C. Convention," *Marian Studies* 27 (1976): 5–10. Report on convention for the MSA by Carol.

"Religious Congregation Honors Mary as Co-redemptrix," *Marianum* 38 (1976): 529–530.

"Dr. J. M. Alonso on Mary's Mediation," *Ephemerides Mariologicae* 26 (1976): 159–167.

"Notas marginales a la respuesta del Padre Alonso," *Ephemerides Mariologicae* 26 (1976): 272–276.

1977

"Report on the North Palm Beach Convention," *Marian Studies* 28 (1977), 5–9. Report on convention for the MSA by Carol.

"The Blessed Virgin and the "Debitum Peccati." A Bibliographical Conspectus," *Marian Studies* 28 (1977), 181–256.

1978

A History of the Controversy over the "Debitum Peccati", Franciscan Institute Publications. Theology Series, No. 9 (St. Bonaventure, NY.: The Franciscan Institute, 1978), xiii, 1–260.

"A Towering Figure," in *P. Carlo Balic, O.F.M. Profilo, impressioni, ricordi, a cura di* P. Paolo Melada, O.F.M., e P. Dinko Aracic, O.F.M., (Roma, Pontificia Accademia Mariana Internazionale, 1978), 136–137.

"Mary's Coredemption in a Petition of the Cuban Hierarchy to Pius XII," *Marianum* 40 (1978), pp. 440–44.

"Report on the Baltimore, Md. Convention," *Marian Studies* 29 (1978): 5–11. Report on convention for the MSA by Carol.

1979

"Reflections on the Problem of Mary's Preservative Redemption," *Marian Studies* 30 (1979): 19–88.

1980

"Memorial Tribute to Cardinal John J. Wright (+ 1979)," *Marian Studies* 31 (1980): 36–39.

"The Absolute Predestination of the Blessed Virgin Mary," *Marian Studies* 31 (1980): 172–238.

1981

The Absolute Primacy and Predestination of Jesus and His Virgin Mother, (Chicago: Franciscan Herald Press, 1981), xiii, 1–177.

Michael Meilach, *Mary Immaculate in the Divine Plan,* The Marian Library, 1 (Wilmington, DE: Glazier, 1981) vi, 1-96. Preface by J. B. Carol, O.F.M., pp. v-vi.

1982

"Cur Deus Homo?" *Homiletic and Pastoral Review* 82 (August-September 1982): 8–9.

1983

"Duns Scotus on the Incarnation," *Homiletic and Pastoral Review* 83 (June 1983): 4.

1984

Francesco Saverio Pancheri, *The Universal Primacy of Christ*, translated and adapted from the Italian edition by J. B. Carol, O.F.M. (Front Royal, Virginia, Christendom 1984), x, 1-144.

1985

"Predestination of Mary," in *Dictionary of Mary: "Behold Your Mother"*, (New York: Catholic Book Publishing Co., 1985), 273–275.

1986

Why Jesus Christ? Thomistic, Scotistic and Conciliatory Perspectives, (Manassas, Virginia, Trinity Communications, 1986), xvii, 1–531.[403]

1990

Holy Name Province, Provincial Office, Letter to the Friars concerning Fr. Carol's passing, April 9, 1990.

1991

Koehler, Theodore A., S.M. "In Homage to the Founder of the Mariological Society of America Juniper Benjamin Carol, O.F.M. (1911-1990), Ephemerides Mariologiae Annus LIII-Fasc. II - n. 142- (1991).

Fr. Juniper Carol. *The Provincial Annals* Vol. 40, 1991 Pg. 109–12.

1992

Fehlner, Peter D. O.F.M.Conv. "Fr. Juniper B. Carol, O.F.M.: His Mariology and Scholarly Achievement." *Marian Studies* Volume 42 (1992). (A write up on Father Carol by Father Fehlner).

2015

Kozack, Jessica Catherine, *The Primacy of Christ as the Foundation of the Coredemption: The Mariology of Fr. Juniper B. Carol, O.F.M. (1911-1990)*. Master's Thesis from University of Dayton, (Aug. 2015).

---

[403] Fr. Gambero puts this under 1985, but Fehlner under 1986. The actual publication date is 1986.